Miss
American
Pie

Miss American Pie

A Diary of Love, Secrets, and Growing Up in the 1970s

Margaret Sartor

BLOOMSBURY

Published by Bloomsbury USA, New York
Distributed to the trade by Holtzbrinck Publishers

Grateful acknowledgment is extended to the following for permission to reprint copyrighted material: "American Pie," by Don McLean. © 1971, renewed 1999 by Music Corporation of America, Inc. and Benny Bird Co., Inc. All rights administered by Songs of Universal, Inc./BMI. Used by Permission. All Rights Reserved. "Down to You," by Joni Mitchell. © 1974 Crazy Cow Music. All rights administered by Sony/ATV Music Publishing, 8 Music Square West, Nashville, TN 37203. All Rights Reserved. Used by Permission. "On the Road to Find Out," by Cat Stevens. © Copyright 1970 (Renewed) by Cat Music Limited. International Copyright Secured. All Rights Reserved. Reprinted by Permission. "Tea for the Tillerman," by Cat Stevens. © Copyright 1970 (Renewed) Salafa Music. International Copyright Secured. All Rights Reserved. Reprinted by Permission. "In this Short life" from *Bolts of Melody: New Poems of Emily Dickinson,* edited by Mabel Loomis Todd and Millicent Todd Bingham. © Copyright 1945 by the Trustees of Amherst College. Copyright renewed 1973 by Katherine Loomis and George Loomis II. Reprinted by permission of HarperCollins Publishers. The quotation from "Lines on a Young Lady's Photograph Album" by Philip Larkin is reprinted from *The Less Deceived* by permission of The Marvell Press, England and Australia.

All papers used by Bloomsbury USA are natural, recyclable products made from wood grown in well-managed forests. The manufacturing processes conform to the environmental regulations of the country of origin.

THE LIBRARY OF CONGRESS HAS CATALOGED THE HARDCOVER EDITION AS FOLLOWS:

Sartor, Margaret.
Miss American pie : a diary of love, secrets, and growing up in the 1970s / Margaret Sartor.—1st U.S. ed.
p. cm.
1. Sartor, Margaret—Childhood and youth. 2. Sartor, Margaret—Diaries. 3. Teenage girls—Louisiana—Montgomery—Diaries. 4. Adolescence—Louisiana—Montgomery. I. Title.

HQ798.S24 2006
305.235'20976309047—dc22
2005030965

First published in the United States by Bloomsbury in 2006
This paperback edition published 2007

Paperback ISBN-10: 1-59691-201-4
ISBN-13: 978-1-59691-201-4

10 9 8 7 6 5 4 3 2 1

Typeset by Westchester Book Group
Printed in the United States of America by Quebecor World Fairfield

This book is for Alex.
Everyone knows why.

All that is included here is based on the diaries, notebooks, and letters I wrote as a girl. Names have been changed to protect the privacy of others, and some sequences and details of events have been rearranged, not in an attempt to obscure the facts, but to better reveal them. Throughout the process of working on this book, the assistance and support of my family and friends has been crucial, and without their trust it would not have been possible.

The obvious is the very last thing we see.

—*Wright Morris*

An Introduction

MONROE, LOUISIANA, isn't a very small town, but it's small enough. In the 1970s, the divorce rate in my hometown was nearly nonexistent, church attendance was roughly 100 percent, and the rules of proper behavior were generally agreed upon, if often ignored. You could be a licensed driver at fifteen and order a double bourbon at eighteen, which meant that we were driving at fourteen and anyone who looked eighteen could buy liquor at 7-Eleven. We purchased cigarettes from vending machines, rode bikes without helmets, and thought seat belts and sunscreen were for wimps. Marijuana was available, but still uncommon. Sex was available, common, and never discussed openly between polite parents and their children. Monroe wasn't a backwater, but it wasn't progressive either. On the whole, I would say my hometown was entirely typical of its time and place, more confused than reactionary, a sort of stronghold of befuddlement.

I grew up on a boulevard lined with live oaks that were ancient and dramatically canopied over the beginning of the road, but dwindled to saplings no taller than my father toward the recently paved end where we lived. Our house was a ramblingly comfortable orangey-red brick ranch in a growing development of one-acre lots carved out of a pre-Civil War cotton plantation along the banks of the Ouachita River. In more ways than one, Monroe and the economy of northeastern Louisiana were built on the black soil of the merging floodplains of the Mississippi and Ouachita rivers, and my childhood home was less than a football field's length from the lesser river's edge. Barges and boats traveled the Ouachita River from Arkansas to the Gulf of Mexico, and water moccasins and alligator gar bred in the shadows of the cypress tree roots along its edge. The river's age and length were unimaginable to me and its depth swelled and shrank according to factors outside my grasp. Inseparable from the Ouachita, then as now, was the levee that snaked beside it like a miniature Great Wall of China, a man-made construction defying scale and logic, stretching, as far as I could tell, forever in both directions. Growing up, I felt I owned them both, or more precisely, I felt that since no one else owned them, the levee and river were always there for me. This is what I think of when I picture my past: the walk out my back door across the brick patio, past the overgrown azaleas and the tall metal swing set, up to the top of the levee and then down into a narrow swath of woods that led to a rise on the riverbank. I liked to sit there and write and watch the last light of day glare and glisten like fool's gold over the fast-moving muddy waters.

In my teenage years, my immediate family—my parents, me, two older sisters, and a younger brother—was stable but less than uniform, a complicated arrangement held together by habit and stubbornness as well as love. My father, a physician, was intelligent, capable, generous, and kind, but he was not a modern man; he did

Dr. Tom Sartor

not discuss his feelings. The rare times Daddy demonstrated strong emotions of any variety are memorable. He never panicked, but under certain circumstances, he lost his temper. I could walk in the back door covered in mud and cradling a broken arm and my father would remain calm, but a boyfriend arriving on a motorcycle would bring his blood to a quick boil. Maybe there was a time in my father's life when he lacked certainty, wasn't comfortable with life-and-death decisions, but I can't imagine it. He was the eldest of three sons, raised on a cotton farm during the Great Depression by a widowed mother who taught elementary school five days a week and Bible study on Sundays. Daddy and his brothers all attended college and medical school on loans and scholarships, then returned to serve the same population in the same hospital and local clinics. To distinguish them from one another, patients and nurses called them by their first names. My father was Dr. Tom.

As much as Daddy was an exemplar of solid citizenry, my mother, Bobbie Sue, was generally viewed as eccentric, a free spirit: someone who never wore anything with a floral motif and always did her own hair. She was also, in the opinion of everyone but herself, drop-dead gorgeous, always at her most beautiful when she made the least effort, which was most of the time. Though she stayed home, I have trouble thinking of my mother as a homemaker. Mama was a decade younger than Daddy, unabashedly volatile, and she could draw and paint with near photographic accuracy. Even then I sensed that being a housewife and mother were roles with inherent limitations that did not naturally suit her. It was her studio, a locked room near the back door of the house, that nurtured her best self. By the time I was a teenager, I finally caught on that at least half the time, Mama only pretended to leave the house so she could crawl back in her studio window to paint undisturbed. My mother was well known for her antics and tricky practicality. She was funny and frank and whistled with her fingers in her mouth, the kind of woman adolescent boys fantasized their girlfriends would grow up to be. For me as a teenage girl, this was both fabulous and often fabulously painful.

Having two older sisters who regularly registered double takes among males of any age was annoying as well. From a purely psychological perspective, it's safe to assume that my being the third daughter, followed by an adorable and troublesome younger brother, added a certain level of frustration to my formative years, a well-founded fear of being overlooked; but then growing up is difficult under the best of circumstances, and these just happened to be mine.

Mrs. Bobbie Sue Sartor

When I began the diary in 1972, my socially gifted oldest sister, Mary, was away at college. The next in line, Stella, whose serious personality was weighted in direct opposition to Mary's buoyancy, was a senior in high school. My distracting younger brother, Bill, was ten years old, and I was in the commonly acknowledged worst year of life, the seventh grade. My parents were attentive, loving, and strict. There were rules, expectations, and consequences. When I screwed up, I always started the confession process with my mother, which was risky and dependent on her mood, but better than conversations with Daddy, which were logical, and therefore hopeless. The end result, in either case, was usually the same: I was sent to my room. When being sent to my room was extended to include days rather than hours, it was called being grounded. About the time I started being grounded, I started writing things down; it gave me something to do. Writing to and for myself had an acceptably low risk factor for feeling misunderstood or ignored, and it was a form of conversation I came to value more and more.

My bedroom, aside from being a place of exile, was also a refuge. The shelves were a cherished disarray of books, vinyl records, magazines, notebooks, and souvenirs. I collected things: books, model horses, rocks, and photographs of Mikhail Baryshnikov and Marilyn Monroe. My walls were an evolving collage of drawings, lists, snapshots, and 4-H ribbons. The decorative centerpiece was a poster above my bed, an image I mulled over daily until it gradually etched itself into my subconscious appearing even in my dreams, my first template of romance and longing: an enlargement of a black-and-white photograph of a young couple standing in a field at sunset, accompanied by a quotation from Frederick S. Perls that read, "You are you, and I am I, and if by chance we find each other, it's so beautiful." Popular music was inseparable from my emotional life and I played records relentlessly. The volume to which I could push my personal angst was, however, strictly limited by the black Rub-a-Dub laundry pen mark Mama drew on the volume dial of my stereo. I remember my mother claiming, loudly and usually while surveying my room from my doorway (in blatant violation of the "do not disturb or die" sign which no one seemed to take seriously and I was powerless to enforce), that my bedroom smelled, and I suppose it did, but it was not disagreeable to me. The faint odors of oiled leather tack, potpourri, paints, candy bars, skin lotion, dog hair, and dirty clothes were all of my own making, and I thought my room was an OK place to be.

On reflection, I think the sediment of memory must resemble that room, and in my initial reading of the diaries there were times that I became aware of those long undisturbed layers of sensory information, images I didn't know I could conjure, feelings I didn't know I still felt. Reading an entry, such as, "Went skiing on the bayou. Mitch kept flirting with me and I kept liking it." and an entire afternoon's experience would suddenly be revealed to me in full: the appalling heat, the relief of the breeze when the boat was in motion, Mitch's extremely short cutoffs and the fact that he wore no underwear. Scratch the surface and the past was there. Heartaches mostly. And the buried hurts and humiliations that hurt and humiliated me all over again.

My First Diary

I HAVE HEARD it said that there are two times in your life when you stand a chance, in the face of whatever social forces struggle to get you in their grip, of becoming someone new, of creating your own personal universe through the sheer power of imagination and persistence: one is adolescence and the other is middle age. Maybe this is hogwash. Maybe it's profound truth. I certainly make no claim to know. What I do know is that very near my forty-third birthday, it dawned on me to look at the diaries I began when I was young. I didn't know how young. I wasn't sure at what age or even why I had started keeping diaries, because scribbling in blank books, tossing them into storage boxes, and hauling them from car trunk to closet, has been a natural part of what I do for so long that I had never, that I could remember, given thought to when it actually became necessary for me to do it.

It was early October, an afternoon shrouded in unreasonable heat, and I was at home writing about a series of pictures I had made, over many years, in my hometown in Louisiana. These were photographs of people I had watched and loved since my first steady gaze, but for the life of me I couldn't find the words to explain my ardent, though not always kind, attention. I wanted to tell the story of my growing up, but just *thinking* about my childhood seemed to ignite an internal battle, to generate, simultaneously, both a meditative sense of calm and considerable irritation. Then it occurred to me that the words weren't in my head. They were in the attic.

Twenty minutes of sweaty excavation among old clothes, holiday decorations, and used camping gear finally yielded pay dirt. There, in the oldest box of various sized books, binders, and bad poetry, I found it: the little red leatherette book, the one with the Greek key border design and the broken binding—my first diary. In a spot directly under a bare lightbulb, I opened it and read, in clumsy penciled words, "January 1, 1972. It rained today. We went to the movies."

I held still, the way you do when you see something unexpected and possibly marvelous in a junk shop, and you know no one else has noticed it yet, but you. Standing in the attic detritus of my adult life, I listened to my husband call my name as he walked in and out the back door with bags of groceries and heard the whoops of my two children competing in a ferocious game of Ping-Pong. My back ached, my period was late, and middle age was descending upon my life like cold rain on a previously cloudless day, yet there I was looking at my own loopy handwriting from the precipice of puberty, before I'd been drunk, kissed, or worn a bra, reading thoughts (such as they were) I'd conceived and written when I was twelve-and-a-half years old. The exact age of my son.

Among other things, like teaching for a living and getting my kids to the dentist twice a year, I make photographs, and sometimes I write, and usually in a way that scrutinizes life, offers up a version of the world that can be beautiful but also can, in its exactness, at times seem cruel. Diaries, on the other hand, are truly cruel. A diary has none of the sweetness of nostalgia and little to do with the sentiments that lock certain moments into the patchwork of the mind's eye to become a memory. A diary is not about the past; it's about the present, a record of precisely what you are getting through or over, trying to savor or avoid, at the very moment you are doing it. If memory stores the spirit of our experiences, then a diary, in its bona fide physical existence, surely retains the flesh and blood.

Some trips are worth a bumpy ride; some vaccinations are worth the risk of lifelong paralysis. I read my diaries. I read six years of them in two days. The earliest ones held few surprises and were somewhat discomfiting, but twelve-year-olds tend to be petty and thirteen-year-olds are usually self-involved. It was the diaries from age fourteen to eighteen that lay beyond tidy generalizations. Not that my adolescence was so different from anyone else's. None of us is prepared for the hormonal heresy of puberty, and each of us finds our own particular way of getting through it. My strategy was to write things down. Whenever I felt trapped or bored and had a pen and a scrap of paper with a decent margin (school handouts, church bulletins, discarded grocery lists, my diary), I wrote, to no one in particular, about what I thought, saw, dreamed of, overheard, worried over, and obsessed upon: God, sex, and the whole messy endeavor of trying to hold my own and create my own identity. If the circumstances of my life got particularly dire, I wrote directly to Jesus.

The charismatic (and where I grew up, common) brand of Christianity into which I was reborn as a teenager was nothing less than my lifeboat, a kind of calm, steady source of reassurance that the creator of the universe was intimately involved with the ongoing struggles of my friendships, my hair, my love life, and the not insignificant concern I had for my family. It also allowed me to cultivate, in my most private self, a species of hope on which I rely still—I learned to pray. Eventually, it was the solace of prayer that gave me the courage necessary to abandon evangelical presumption, a leap that is not for the weak of heart. It was still some time before I began to understand that life is not inherently noble, that dignity is not guaranteed by piety, and that love, though the greatest of human virtues, is also the most elusive and inextricably connected to loss. How long did that take? Years. A blink. The whole of my life.

IN A TOWN LIKE MONROE, children form bonds early and usually according to age, neighborhood, and how your family spends its free time. When I was growing up, loyalties shifted subtly from year to year, or sometimes week to week, but we were the same friends at eighteen that we were at age seven. We ate at the same burger joints, swam in the same backyard pools, attended the same birthday parties, and joined the same church youth groups. And we were all white.

Some people, including my own children, have the mistaken idea that when the U.S. Supreme Court ruled on Brown v. Board of Education in 1954, things began to change. They didn't. Not for a very long time and never in the ways that they could have. By the 1970s, the public schools in Monroe were beginning to integrate, but cultural segregation remained as distinct as the railroad tracks that divided the white side of town from its mirror community of churches, homes, and shops on the black side. In the economically dominant white neighborhood where I lived, the emblems of the defeated Confederacy were ubiquitous and accorded a reverence similar to the heroics of Washington and the miseries of Job—making it very difficult to grasp the South's morally corrupt past. The black kids who sat next to me in the first integrated classrooms at Robert E. Lee Junior High surely had a wholly different view of our overlapping history and well understood the tinderbox of the historic moment we shared, but in the diaries, it is shockingly clear that I did not. Following the lead of my parents, I was naively optimistic, not only about desegregation, but about the country in general, a luxury afforded me by the color of my skin and my family's economic security. At my house, history was discussed, but never politics. I was raised believing that good always won out, that anti-Semitism died with Hitler, and prejudice was an immature attitude that people were bound to outgrow. It was only after I left home, and Monroe, that I began to understand how little I understood about so much. I did have my moment of revelation about racial divisions and distrust in the American South, but it did not happen while I was in high school.

I wrote a lot about boys. Attraction, sex, desire, rejection, love, and loneliness were preoccupations, and quite a few boys moved in and out of my at first nonexistent and then weirdly elastic romantic reach. There were nonstarters like Cliff and Vernon, then the smooth-talking Tony, my buddy Edgar Napoleon, the delinquent Beau, the offending Chris, and the seductive Dash. There was, of course, Mitch, the flirtatious boy in the boat, who was bright and swaggering, with unruly dark hair and a winning grin. He captured my eye early on and later, a piece of my heart. And the only boyfriend besides Mitch who mattered was Jackson Bishop.

I was not the only person crazy in love with Jackson. He was tall and towheaded and had warm brown eyes with a mesmerizing effect on girls and boys alike. When I first met Jackson, I was fourteen with a full set of braces on my teeth, and he was sixteen and already had a coterie of current and ex-girlfriends. He could play the piano as well as he played fullback; he wore blue-and-white checkered platform shoes, quoted Frost, and was fervently devoted to his dog. Jackson was not only popular, he was out of the ordinary. He was also a close friend of the boy I considered my oldest friend, my next-door neighbor Tommy.

Tommy Townsend and I grew up in each other's kitchens, privy to our mothers' gossip and ordering our younger brothers around like ancillary staff. We had mutual childhood serial obsessions: bird nests, Barbie dolls, chemistry sets, and the migration paths of butterflies. By high school, Tommy was over six feet tall, but he didn't care for rough sports, killing deer, or driving Broncos in the mud. He was friendly and a little goofy, though no goofier than I, only friendlier. Because Tommy was a grade ahead of me in school, we were never in the same classes, and outside of our mutual affection for Jackson, we tended to keep other friendships separate. Ours was a familiarity born in the boredom of summer afternoons and cemented in the sneaky behavior of the night. At the end of the day, we were never farther apart than a walk across the driveway.

Pam, Wanda, Betsy, and Angela were the girlfriends with whom I was bunched daily in carpools and classrooms. Pam was the tallest and loudest, the only girl in the eighth grade who polished her shoes, painted her fingernails, and cussed like a fighter pilot. She was also the only person I knew with divorced parents, the closest thing to worldly sophistication that I was exposed to until college. Pam's mother's household was familiarly strict, but at her father's home, we snuck swigs of bourbon and gawked at *Playboy* magazines unsupervised. Wanda, who introduced me to

My cousin Clara and Tommy and me in my bedroom

the magic of black light and Bill Withers, had impressively curvy hips. Once, while her parents were away on vacation, she painted her entire bedroom lime green. I didn't get to know Betsy well until high school. She was a year older, slim and pretty, and walked with the upright posture and turned-out feet of a dancer. Rare among teenagers, Betsy had an unyielding hopefulness.

We all laughed a lot, but only Angela laughed gently. She tucked her chin, lowered her eyes, and chuckled. I loved Angela in a more complicated way than I did the rest of my girlfriends. Maybe, or maybe not, because we were blood relatives, our mothers were sisters and we shared a grandmother—Momma Doll. Angela's mother, my Aunt Lou, had moods that swung on a long rope with a tentative link to real events. When Aunt Lou wasn't raucous or eager to go shopping, she was wringing her hands and walking the floor. Angela, by contrast, was unrivaled in her modesty and discipline. She made excellent grades, counted her calories, kept her tan even, and planned her outfits to the smallest accessory. Everything I know about hairspray, perfume, tampons, and panty hose, I learned from my cousin Angela.

During the early part of high school, I belonged to a prayer group. These purposeful gatherings were my first exposure to serious discussion and debate over questions of truth, spirituality, and moral intention, and I was entranced. Moreover, I was enraptured by the emotionality that we, as a group, could generate. But the arc of my spiritual life did not begin in that prayer group, or in any other sort of group. It began in the woods, while I was alone and usually on horseback.

Angela, me (with Rex), and my cousin Ann on the levee behind my house

Parts of the hundreds of acres of woods behind my home were as well known to me as the streets and backyards of my neighborhood, but since the forest lay in the undeveloped floodplain of the river and surrounding bayous, the land was constantly being altered and reshaped by the change of seasons and corresponding rise and fall of water. Candy, a gentle paint mare, was my first pony and I rode her bareback because in those early elementary school years I was too small to lift a saddle on my own. When I was in the eighth grade, I inherited Rex, a handsome sorrel-colored gelding, from my older sister Stella, who had gone off to college. Rex was taller and stronger than the average horse, and faster, too. He had a wide white blaze and black eyes that could register intense curiosity, fear, and mischief. He was easily bored and wickedly smart. It is the miracle of animal domestication that a puny adolescent girl could control, even dominate, a horse like Rex, but as any rider will tell you, that control could not have existed without mutual trust and constant communication. I spent uncountable hours for many years roaming, inspecting, and exploring the woods on Candy or Rex, and always with my sad-eyed black-and-tan mutt named Honey running close behind. Sometimes I rode in a headlong rush, sometimes with cultivated patience. At times I lost myself in awe. This is why, in the diary, I write about talking to my horses and feeling understood. Because there were defining moments in my life that I shared with only those animals. Because it was in the woods with my horse and my dog where the searching began, and where the question of God first rose in my body as easy as breath.

THE STORY MY DIARIES TELL is a quarter century gone. It's not complicated, dramatic, or epic, but things happened. Set against the backdrop of the Deep South in the 1970s, fundamentalist Christianity, school desegregation, sexual revolution, and the invention of childproof caps, it is still only my story, my teetering teenage sanity hanging in the balance of ordinary daily decisions, good and bad luck. And though my adolescence was particular, it was certainly not unique. With so many things happening for the first time, teenagers are well aware of the intensity of their feelings, but most are unable to grasp the long-lasting influence those feelings wield. Science and the adult world, however, know the seminal power of teenage emotion to be plain, road-tested, biological fact. And we even know why. We know that in those outrageously prolonged adolescent years, of what we only later recognize to be brief and fast-moving lives, it is precisely in the *not knowing* that our emotions have their power, their risk of ruin, and the potential to set us free.

My Cast of Characters

Mrs. Bobbie Sue Sartor	Mama
Dr. Tom Sartor	Daddy
Mary	my oldest sister
Stella	my next older sister
Bill	my younger brother
Momma Doll	maternal grandmother
Tommy Townsend	my next-door neighbor
Ellen Townsend	Tommy's mother
Aunt Lou	my mother's only sister
Angela	my cousin, Aunt Lou's daughter
Pam, Wanda, and Betsy	the rest of the girlfriends
Mitch Hardy	boyfriend
Jackson Bishop	the other boyfriend
Chris, Dash, Tony, Edgar Napoleon (E.N.)	some of the boys

That this is a real girl in a real place,

In every sense empirically true!
Or is it just *the past*?

—*Philip Larkin,*
from "Lines on a Young Lady's Photograph Album"

1972

"It wasn't my hair. It was a tree."

January 1
It rained today. We went to the movies.

January 2
Rained again. That's my life.

January 3
My name is Margaret Earline Sartor. I'm in the seventh grade at Robert E. Lee Junior High in Monroe, Louisiana, the United States of America, the Earth, the Universe. I am bored out of my mind.

January 4
Joey broke up with Pam. She cried a lot.

January 5
Cut my hair in a shag.

January 8
Honey had 9 puppies.

January 16
The shag isn't working.

January 17
Candy and Rex loose again. Am making a quirt.

January 18
Quirt broke. I'm going to make a bat.

January 20
Found four beer cans in the woods near the Indian Mound.

January 22

Wanda said Mike kissed her. Mike is this real old guy that has a horse at the stables and he rode with Wanda out in the woods and grabbed her.

January 24

Puppies opened eyes. I wish I had a best friend.

January 26

I'm going to make a table out of old beer cans.

January 28

After dinner Daddy sat down and played the piano. He played *Beethoven!* I didn't even know he knew *how* to play the piano. I don't feel too good.

January 30

I might be sick.

February 2

It hurts when I breathe. Daddy says I might have a lung disease.

February 3

Mama won't let me go riding because of the disease I might have.

February 4

Clothilde came over to borrow milk and she said someone in her church died from a lung disease. Daddy says I have pleurisy and no one dies from it and it will go away if I take it easy and not complain.

February 8
I am completely fine but Mama doesn't believe me. I hate this.

February 10
Tomorrow I go riding.

February 17
Cliff acts like he likes me because he talks to me a lot.

February 19
Bought a get-well card for Susie. She might go deaf.

February 21
Gave away puppies and my old teacher Mrs. Parks got Bobby Lou.
She changed his name to Snoopy.

February 22
Daddy says he plays the trombone and the lyre. I had to look up
lyre in the encyclopedia.

February 24
The worst part about school is standing in the lunch line because
all the girls flirt with boys or stand with their best friend & snob
other girls.

February 28
Cheerleader tryout practice today. I hope I get it. (I know I
won't.)

March 1
A boy threw up in class.

March 2

Mrs. Tolliver has ESP and told us things we were thinking.

March 6

Didn't make the 8 finalists for cheerleader but Pam and Mary Ann did. Came home and made cookies.

March 7

Four girls were elected cheerleader. Everyone thinks they only picked four to keep Mary Ann off the squad because she's black.

March 8

Got school annuals and a lot of people signed mine. Iona wrote "Do you have soul? Yes, you have soul." Mary Ann wrote, "To one of my best white friends."

March 9

Pam wrote in my annual, "I love you but I can do without you." Cliff gave me a picture of himself.

March 10

In chorus, Mrs. Tolliver always points to my side of the room and says that someone in that area is off and everyone looks at me.

March 13

Mama got so mad after dinner that she threw a wet dish towel at Bill and walked out of the kitchen crying. Bill was joking and said something that did it, but I couldn't tell what it was.

March 15

Pam likes Angela and I think they are getting to be best friends.

March 16
I don't like Pam anymore.

March 17
The new cheerleaders asked me to be the mascot next year. I have to dress up like an eagle with feathers and everything. It's good but I don't know why they picked me.

March 18
Everyone was nice to me today.

March 19
The photographer came to take our family portrait and Daddy wouldn't let Honey be in the picture because he thinks she's ugly. Taffy got to be in the picture because he's a cocker spaniel.

March 20
Pam told Angela she thought I hated her. Shit.

March 22
Rode Candy. Ran all through the woods and almost fell off 20 times bareback.

March 28
Today I was feeding the horses and ate some oats to see what they tasted like. They don't taste so good.

April 10
I have no boobs. My teeth are buck and my hair is frizzy. I look like a Q-tip.

April 16
Apollo 16 blastoff.

April 17
I like Cliff but Pam told me he only likes whores.

April 19
Gail is breaking up with Gary. He said her pussy was as big as a horse's. Stayed home and embroidered.

April 21
Daddy told Stella that if he caught her sneaking out, he would lock the door and she couldn't come back. We had catfish for supper.

April 23
Pam is good at gymnastics but I am better.

April 25
Did 52 sit-ups today. Angela went to a funeral.

April 26
Cliff acts so nice to me.

April 27
Philcivole means I love Cliff in code.

April 29
Jumped 6'2" for standing broad jump. Finished the book about Jim Thorpe.

April 30
Have read all the biographies in the school library. My favorite was the one about Samuel Clemens (Mark Twain).

May 2
Been smoking lately but decided to give it up.

May 3
Math is stupid.

May 5
I understand Math.

May 7
Philcivole (I think).

May 8
Tried to get Candy used to pulling a sack full of cans but she is scared to death of it.

May 9
Went to the library with Pam. She wanted to go across the street to the Quickie Mart and we did and then Mama came early & caught us. Mama is so mad she said I can't go back to the library for a year. (I just wanted to read horse magazines.)

May 10
I think Cliff is acting nicer to me.

May 11
While I was walking down the hall, I heard somebody say Cliff liked me.

May 18

Found out they may not use a sack of cans in the trail riding class. (I practiced it.)

May 19

Today at the stables Pam told me if I wanted to get into her "Do It Yourself Club" I had to go tell Wanda I was cuter and sweeter and all this crap and I did it. Then Pam told Wanda she had to throw dirt in Angela's hair and dunk her in the water trough and she did it. Then me and Angela and Wanda went swimming and decided that Pam is full of shit.

May 29

Waited all day for Angela to call me and she didn't. Rearranged room.

June 1

Mailed 12 entries to VitaGloss contest in *Horse and Rider* magazine.

June 2

Got braces on bottom teeth. (If he had stabbed me in the gums with a knife it would have hurt less.)

June 5

Mr. Hern drove the bus route backwards.

June 10

Mama says I don't need a bra. If she thinks I'm going to go another year to P.E. without a bra, she's crazy.

June 12

Mike knocked down all the bird nests at the stables. I brought a baby bird home and named him Corky. He eats dog food.

June 13

Corky was killed by a dog. I loved her.

June 15

Mother is making me take sewing lessons at the Singer store in the mall. In the first class we had to strip to our underwear so the teacher could take our measurements.

June 16

In sewing lesson we had to strip *again* to try on the patterns.

June 20

Skipped sewing lesson. Went to a movie.

June 22

Mama took me to buy a bra at Welty's Dress Shop and it was HORRIBLE! Old Mrs. Welty kept talking to me through the slats in the dressing room door and asking if it fit and Mama was talking so loud that everyone in the shoe area could hear! From now on, I'm only shopping at *Sears*.

June 24

Found a kitten in our yard and named him Cupcake. He sleeps in a basket by my bed.

June 25

Mama and I got in a big fight. Kitten ran all over everywhere.

June 26

Gave the kitten to the vet, then came home and cried.

July 1

Spent the night with Wanda and a bunch of boys came over. We were all talking outside and Tony sat by me, so Wanda got mad because she likes Tony. Now I like Tony but I'm afraid to tell Wanda.

July 3

A 111 year old lady in our church died yesterday. I thought she was already dead.

July 13

I was at Wanda's and we were listening to her Bill Withers record ("Lean On Me" is my *favorite* song) and I thought I was getting sick because my stomach started hurting, but I went to the bathroom and my underwear was all *brown* (I thought it would be *red*) and I realized I had started my period!! I stuffed my underwear full of toilet paper and didn't tell Wanda and I went home. Mama gave me a belt and a Kotex pad and some aspirin and now I'm having cramps and feel like I'm wearing a diaper.

July 14

Candy is limping again. Getting poison ivy. Wish I had a drink.

July 15

Switched hiding place of diary. Taking pills to stop itching of poison ivy.

July 16

George the dog got hold of a kitten. I took it to Dr. Cummings and he put it to sleep because two legs & its backbone were broken.

July 17
I found another cat & kittens at the stables and brought them home so George wouldn't get them.

July 23
Wore a halter top today. Bought a new bra.

July 25
My parents told me I could change to River View (the new white school) if I wanted but I don't. Tommy Townsend next door says he might have to.

July 27
I remember exactly when Martin Luther King, Jr., was killed because I was in the kitchen and Mrs. Stringfellow from down the street was there and she said, "Maybe it's for the best" and Mama made me go outside.

July 30
There was a picture in the paper of a wood statue of the Virgin Mary in New Orleans with tears in her eyes and her nose dripping. I taped it on the wall in my room.

August 1
The squirrel died and I buried her in the horse pen.

August 4
Pam made fun of me in front of Tommy Townsend because I was swishing my spit without realizing it. I got mad and Pam said I'm too serious by half. She can be such a *pissbutt*.

— *1972* —

August 9
Today *everyone* was angry. Mama was angry at Stella and Mary, who were angry at each other. Mama was angry at Daddy because he didn't care enough about who was angry. Daddy left and Stella started crying and Mary went outside and slammed the door. Mama made a racket in the kitchen. Bill went to his room and read comic books. I *hated* it.

August 10
Stella left for college today and Mary leaves for college in a week. At dinner, Momma Doll said, "My granddaughters are growing up too fast." (It doesn't seem too fast to me.)

August 11
Wanda spent the night. We drank vodka, gin, bourbon with Tab. My parents never notice because I pour a little bit out of each bottle. I heard Mama say that the newspaper said that President Nixon says the war in Vietnam is over.

August 12
I'm 13 years old—officially a teenager. Got a set of heat rollers.

August 13
We had a garage sale at our house and I made $2.05. Mary made $60.

August 14
Mary and Stella have baby books with lots of pictures and writing. My baby book has only three pictures and Bill doesn't even have a baby book. That's why I tell him he's adopted.

August 15
Rode with Pam in the woods & had two glasses of vodka and orange juice. (screwballs)

August 16
Mary's boyfriend Riley is here to pick her up to take her back to college. We all like him. He's going to visit here for a few days and sleep on the living room sofa.

August 17
After dinner Daddy set up the movie projector and showed old family movies. Mary was so embarrassed in front of Riley that she went to her room and cried but Daddy didn't notice. I thought the movies were funny. Up until the sixth grade, I was a really cute kid.

August 20
I think I like E.N. (His real name is Edgar Napoleon.)

August 22
First day of 8th grade at Robert E. Lee Junior High. I was introduced at assembly as the new mascot but I didn't have to wear the costume. I have a good schedule—except *mean* old Mrs. Potts.

August 23
Saw E.N. but I didn't talk to him because I couldn't think of anything to say.

August 24
Daddy took piano lessons for NINE years! He said his mother made Uncle Henry take violin lessons, but Uncle Henry hated it. So one day Uncle Henry got so fed up he smashed his violin to pieces and that was that.

August 26
Rode Rex. He reared and acted bad and I could hardly control him.
Storm warnings were out.

September 1
At the Monroe High football game there was a Jesus freak out on
the track praying for everyone and people were making fun of
him. I felt sorry for him.

September 4
The Townsends ate supper with us. Tommy came in my room and
talked. He told me that a couple of years ago, when he was about
twelve, his mother told him to stop playing with me all the time
and make friends with other boys, so he did, and that's the reason
we quit being best friends. What I don't understand is why nobody
ever told *me*?

September 5
The cheerleaders asked me to go with them to get their uniforms
but they mostly ignored me. They were surprised at how tall I got
over the summer. One of them said that I'm out of proportion.

September 6
Didn't ride today. Don't know why.

September 7
After practice today the cheerleaders told me not to stay for practice next week.

September 8
I bought the wrong kind of notebook for Mrs. Potts' class and she
had a hissy fit. I think she hates me.

September 11
When Pam told me she liked E.N. I could have cried.

September 13
Pam talked to E.N. before homeroom. She *knows* it's killing me.

September 18
Stayed after school and went over assembly with the cheerleaders who were nicer to me today (sort of).

September 19
Assembly pretty good. I wore my costume and the cheerleaders pulled me in on a red wagon they had decorated. I was so *embarrassed.*

September 20
Today I got out of the car and glanced at my reflection in the windshield and thought—my hair looks awful! Then I looked closer and realized it wasn't my hair, it was a tree.

September 21
E.N. talks to me sometimes.

September 23
Today Pam and Angela said they were going to nap in my room while I was riding. But when I came back to get my hat I found them hunting by my bed (for my diary)—I walked out and rode off. Damn the fuckers!

September 24
Saw Pam and Angela (said nothing about yesterday).

September 25
Found three baby mice in my feed bucket.

September 28
Today a mouse chased me in the tack room and I jumped off a bale of hay and hit my head on a rafter and almost knocked myself unconscious.

October 1
Pam told me Eddie Owens sucked Darlene Cornett's tits.

October 2
Rode way back in the woods in the swamp and it was freezing. I told Rex everything.

October 4
Everyone knows I like E.N. and everyone thinks E.N. likes Pam. I don't think E.N. likes Pam but Tony likes Pam. I think Pam is a bitch.

October 7
Painted rocks.

October 13
Sleepover pallet party at Wanda's. Some girls played Truth or Dare and Julie took a dare to do a cheer *naked* and she did it with pom-poms (gross). Pam asked Darlene if Eddie Owens had sucked her tits and she said yes. I had a stomachache so didn't play.

October 14
Mama made me a sack supper and I ate in the woods by the river with Rex and Honey.

October 18

I feel pretty good, sort of nothing. I never see E.N. anymore.

October 26

I made a bad mistake on my math test. The Eaglettes are going to wear pumpkin heads in the new half-time routine.

October 28

Bitchass (I mean Pam) is going with E.N.

October 29

My cousin Robert is getting married so he brought over all his model airplanes & gave them to Bill. Robert made every one of those planes from kits with glue and tweezers & he had them hanging from the ceiling of his bedroom from *invisible* wires so they looked like they were flying around his room—like *magic*.

October 30

Mama caught Bill having pretend dog fights with Rob's model airplanes & now they are almost all smashed to pieces and she is crying. What she doesn't understand is that Bill *likes* to break things.

October 31

Mama and Daddy got mad because I came in late from Halloween and they grounded me.

November 1

Mama said at breakfast we have to sell Candy. I cried all morning at school.

November 2

Angela's horse JuJu kicked Candy and Candy bucked me off and kicked Spot and Spot threw my cousin Ann. Spot is the ugliest pony I've ever seen. He looks like a big pinto pig.

November 3

Rex was too frisky to ride today.

November 4

I don't think it's strange to kiss your horse on the mouth.

November 5

A boy who lives down the street has been going all over the neighborhood handing out flyers for George McGovern for president. He's not even old enough to vote.

November 6

We sold Candy for $150 to a family just down the road so I'll still be able to visit her.

November 7

E.N. looks so sad to me. He's never with Pam (glad). I love him.

November 8

Nixon was elected president.

November 9

Everyone says me and Vernon would make a good couple.

November 10

Two girls at school have my new dress so now I can't wear it. Mama says she's going to make me. If she does, I'll run away from home.

November 12
Saw movie *Gone with the Wind* for four hours. Now I have a headache. Rhett Butler reminded me of Rex. Can people be like horses?

November 17
Mrs. Tolliver got mad at me for laughing during chorus rehearsal and now I have to sit next to Eddie who is a greaser.

November 18
Rex bucked me off. Hurt my butt.

November 19
I don't know why Angela has been getting on my nerves.

November 20
My butt still hurts.

November 24
A boy with bright red hair and freckles all over named Chick Jones came over to the house and said he was a friend of Stella's. He stayed so long that Mama started cooking dinner anyway. Daddy came home & asked him to leave and he finally did. Then Daddy called Stella and Stella said she'd heard that Chick had dropped out of college because he had a nervous breakdown. His real name is Chickasaw.

December 9
Smoked in the horse pen. Felt queer. Later, a car almost hit me.

December 17
Sat in the woods all day.

December 21
Stayed inside.

December 24
I hate these days with nothing to do.

December 25
Got a new red halter and lead rope and malted milk balls and socks. Ate dinner at Momma Doll's and watched *The Wizard of Oz* on TV.

December 26
Stella said she was going to ride Rex today and then she didn't and I had to sit around all day for nothing.

December 27
Didn't do anything.

December 28
Afraid to ask anyone over. Don't know why.

December 29
Ralph, a kitten I like, is gone from the stables. I hope he's not dead.

December 31
Shot firecrackers about 10:30 p.m. with Tommy. (Shit. Nothing to drink.)

1973

"Please excuse Margaret for not having her pom-poms."

January 1
My New Year's resolutions are to try not to fight with my parents and to make my Daddy cheese and crackers.

January 2
Mama has laryngitis and can't talk. This happens every year.

January 3
A puzzle—try to draw a line to each letter from each dot without crossing lines. (It's possible.)

• • •
C W G

January 5
Crazy Chick Jones showed up again and this time he sat on the couch next to Mama and tried to hold her hand! She asked him to leave and he wouldn't, so Mama told me to go in the bedroom and "ock-lay" the door and sent Bill next door to the Townsends' to call the "olice-pay" (like crazy people can't understand pig latin). The police came and Chick still wouldn't leave, so they had to pick him up off the couch and carry him out to the police car. I heard him tell the police we were his good friends. Snow predicted for this week.

January 7
It snowed & sleeted & everything froze. Electricity went on & off and now it's back on. Trees are coated in ice & falling down every minute. It sounds like gunshots. A tree fell over the horse pen fence. It's so beautiful.

January 8
Day went by so fast. I loved it.

January 10
Sledded down the levee on big sheets of cardboard.

January 11
School tomorrow. Shit.

January 12
A girl I know from church camp is dying.

January 13
A boy I thought was nice (he isn't) is following me around. The creeps always pick me.

January 14
Started period. Feel pretty bad.

January 15
Felt so bad I came home from school.

January 16
Checked out of school after second period, threw up and went back for fifth and sixth period. I feel doomed.

January 22
Melanie invited me to her party but didn't invite Pam and Angela. I hate crap like this.

January 23
Went by Logan Elementary to visit Mrs. Parks. There are more black kids this year but she and Mrs. Smith are still the only black teachers. Mrs. Parks said Snoopy jumped in her bathtub.

January 24

100 on History. Made 78 on English but the *reason* is Mr. Towns took up the test after only 40 minutes! I HATE Mr. Towns. I love Vernon.

January 25

I *want* to be happy but I'm not.

January 26

I want to be happy and love God but I don't know how.

January 27

Spent the night with Wanda. We did tests and found out we have ESP. Cooked a cake and put a fever thermometer in it and the mercury blew up.

January 28

I went to church youth group because I wanted to see E.N. but he wasn't there. A college girl named Brenda testified and talked about finding peace and direction in your life. When I got home I cried.

January 30

Gave a speech in front of English class and Mr. Towns said I looked like I was dancing.

January 31

Missed the school bus so I rode the city bus instead. It cost 15 cents but it was neat. Clothilde rides the bus, but she got off when I got on.

February 1

E.N. said he would kick my ass if I didn't ride the school bus. I like E.N. I can't help it.

February 2

Coach Winky told us if we went to the basketball game we wouldn't have a History test tomorrow & if we didn't, we would. So I went.

February 5

In English class, Gary (jerk) grabbed a poem I was writing from my desk! I grabbed it back and tore it up. The poem started with "I feel so lost" and he read it *out loud!* I feel *stupid!* And really *really* bad.

February 6

Bad headache today.

February 7

Had the heaves.

February 8

Head hurt so bad I couldn't look at anything. Slept all day & hardly ate.

February 10

Felt better today. But I can't stop thinking about what happened with my stupid poem.

February 12

Finally went to school at noon. I'm worried because I have so much work to make up. Placement tests are tomorrow.

February 13
Took placement tests. They were pretty hard.

February 14
No boy on earth will *ever* like me. I told Mama I will never give her grandchildren so she better get used to the idea.

February 15
How do you know which way to turn your head when you kiss so your noses won't bump? I tried kissing Mama's Styrofoam wig head but it felt dumb.

February 17
Ernest the yardman has a crush on Stella & when he's here, he asks me a hundred times when she's coming home and says how pretty she is. People always say how pretty my sisters and my mother are. People used to say I looked like Mama, but they don't anymore.

February 18
Bill was pretending to be Evel Knievel & tried to jump his bike over a ditch and skinned himself up and almost had to get stitches. I do not understand Bill.

February 20
Called Mama to pick me up at school after chorus practice but she forgot until 5:00 p.m. I was the only one there & school locked up when she came. No riding for me.

February 22
E.N. said "Hi Buck" to me today.

March 1
I hate my buck teeth. I love Edgar Napoleon.

March 4
Aunt Lou showed me & Angela her wedding dress. It's made of ivory satin and Angela wants to wear it when she gets married. I asked Mama about her wedding dress and she said she dyed it black to wear to cocktail parties and she doesn't know what happened to it.

March 6
Mama is shitty crazy about TV and won't let me watch anything! She said she only keeps the TV because of Walter Cronkite.

March 10
Rained all day. Reading *Flowers for Algernon.* It depresses me.

March 16
Dr. Cummings came this morning to see Rex's hoof which is cracked and it was raining so he took me to school in his old blue truck. I've decided I want to be a vet like Dr. Cummings and raise horses and maybe dogs, but not cows.

March 18
Pam would hate me if she knew I liked E.N., which makes me sick but I love him.

March 19
Bob the blacksmith said Rex is too hard to shoe and he won't do it. (I know some cowboy beat the shit out of Rex and that's why he doesn't trust men and wants to kill them. I don't blame him. I don't trust them either.)

March 20

There is too much on my mind.

March 21

I feel funny right now. Or it's more like I don't know how I feel.

March 22

School yearbooks came today. I like everything except my mascot picture because I look like a big chicken.

March 23

I don't know why Pam thinks I should like Vernon when he hates me or at least he never talks to me.

March 24

Pam wrote in my annual, "You were always smart in every class. You make me sick." Vernon wrote, "To a good history student." I'm in a very bad mood.

March 25

In a bad mood still. I'm going to do a report on the Ku Klux Klan.

March 27

Anderson Parker wrote in my yearbook "To a real sweet girl that I love a lot." So I kind of like Anderson now but I'm so mixed up I think I LIKE EVERYONE!

March 29

I heard Anderson Parker likes Sherry Smith.

April 2

Had a 98 percentile on the placement test which is very good because Principal Harvey called me especially into his office to tell me.

April 3
I am so *sick* of teachers who say I don't work up to my potential.
I'm sure if you threw water on old Mrs. Potts, she would melt.

April 5
This whore in seventh grade likes Anderson. He sat with her on
the bus but I'm sure he doesn't like her.

April 7
Daddy had an attack of vertigo & had to stay in bed so I sat with
him. Daddy was exactly my age when his father died. I asked why
his father died and Daddy said he was sick. I asked what he was
sick from and Daddy said he didn't know.

April 9
Made 90 on History test but I knew *everything*. Coach Winky asked
stupid questions.

April 11
Taught Rex how to shake hands. I'm going to teach him to lie down.

April 12
Bob the blacksmith finally came and trimmed Rex's hooves. He
had some asshole cowboy with him who put a twitch on Rex's lip
and twisted the chain so tight, I wanted to hit him. If he'd done it
any tighter, I would have *had* to hit him.

April 14
Caught tadpoles. Took them to Mrs. Parks but they died.

April 15
Bill can say his ABCs in burping.

April 16
Went early to school to work on my story for Mr. Towns but it's no good.

April 17
Turned in my story. It's about a boy who goes hunting because his father wants him to go. The boy hates it and he knows his father knows he hates it but they go anyway and then the boy gets sick. (This really did happen to Tommy Townsend. He told me.)

April 18
The river is above flood stage and still rising.

April 20
Mr. Towns liked my story. I'm so happy!

April 21
Mother took me shopping & I couldn't find a single bathing suit that looked halfway decent on me. Mama kept saying how she had terrible acne at my age and I'm so lucky that I don't have acne. It was horrible.

April 22
At Sunday school I felt bad. M. W. K. Got scared. Worse lately. I worry if I can't stop thinking these things, they'll come true. Walked down to see Candy after church and talked to her a long time.

April 23
Daddy said his mother Miss Earline (who I'm named after) was a very smart and religious person. Mama says she was Gandhi-like, only Baptist.

April 24

Daddy's mother didn't believe in working on Sunday so she cooked Sunday dinner on Saturday and when Daddy was little he could play on Sunday but he couldn't dig because that was work.

April 25

The whole eighth grade from Robert E. Lee toured Monroe High today. My group's guide was a sophomore named Cassie Wallace and she wore a bow tie. She's the most interesting girl I've ever seen.

April 26

The river is really high.

April 27

The river is so high it's in the horse pen, so we hauled Rex to a cow pasture in Alto.

April 29

A girl fell in the river and got caught on a tree. She hung on for twenty minutes until someone in a boat saved her.

May 1

Ernest planted turnips in the corner of our yard without asking Mama because he knows Stella loves turnip greens.

May 4

Daddy drove me out to Alto to ride Rex. We went to Gilley's Store and got a Coke and Daddy told me that when he was a kid and worked at the store, there was this one man with six sons who would come in every week for supplies and always used one dime to buy two Coca-Colas. The boys would stand in a circle & pass the Cokes around & each take one swallow until they were empty. (I got a bad sunburn.)

May 5
Pam threw dirt on my sunburn so I hid her books.

May 9
After school Pam asked Angela if she needed a ride and didn't ask me.

May 10
Math test very hard and so I was tardy for Mrs. Potts's class because I tried to finish it. Now Mrs. Potts is making me come to school early tomorrow & Monday. I don't know what it is about me that bothers Mrs. Potts so much.

May 12
Out on the Sartor farm in Alto, there is a family who lives in a trailer home under the bridge. They're squatters. They hunt deer and trap nutria and that's how they make their living. Daddy goes down there every once in awhile to say hello, and he said the last time he went, there were deer heads thrown in the yard for the dogs to chew on. He says they don't bother us and we don't bother them.

May 14
A girl in my class is moving away and at school today she couldn't stop crying. She said everyone in Atlanta has long hair & smokes marijuana.

May 15
Crazy Chick Jones showed up but his father came and took him home. Mama said Chick told her that while he was walking down the street to our house, a city bus flew over his head.

May 19
Miss Illinois won Miss U.S.A.

May 20
Went riding but started feeling bad and went home. I DREAD THIS WEEK.

May 21
I feel sick.

May 22
Stayed home from school today. Am missing the review and it will make the tests harder.

May 23
Felt better this morning, but I was so bored. All that is on TV is Watergate hearings.

May 31
Started menstruating at just the wrong time with swimming party two days away.

June 2
Taped myself up in a plastic bag and went to the swimming party. I want to go to the Sadie Hawkins dance but I don't know what boy to ask.

June 3
Tommy told me to ask his good friend Thad Brown to the dance so I did and he said yes. I'm so relieved! Angela asked Victor Green but he's going out of town. Wanda is going to ask Eddie but I think she is crazy if she does.

June 7
Mama is making me take art lessons. We are doing value studies and I can't do it & Pam can.

June 8
Thad picked me up for the dance at 7:30 and we drove around. We doubled-dated with my cousin Clara and Buddy Regal (the senator's son). We went to eat at El Don José's but left because no one was hungry. Finally we ate at Burger King & everyone got a Coke except Buddy, who already had some beer. At the dance I was scared at first because so many people were drunk, but then I had fun. Thad kissed me good night—a peck. (wow)

June 9
Secretariat won Belmont & Triple Crown by 31 lengths.

June 10
I beat Angela at Ping-Pong.

June 14
Went to art lesson and did dot pictures. Teacher thought mine was one of the best.

June 15
Gail said Darlene's father tried to make out with her at Darlene's house.

June 16
Last art lesson. Hooray! I hate this crap!!!

June 17
Painted my toenails black.

June 19
I think Pam and Angela are mad at me. I try not to be bitchy but then I don't even like me.

June 22
Pam likes E.N., Anderson, and Thad—they all have cars.

June 28
Mama heard that Cassie Wallace is pregnant but I don't believe it.

July 1
I can say the Greek alphabet in less than six seconds. I'm teaching myself to write backwards in cursive.

July 2
Bill found an arrowhead at the Indian Mound, which is where the Ouachita Indians buried their dead all in one spot on top of one another with all their valuables. Daddy made him put it back.

July 4
Angela started her period but went swimming anyway. I don't see how people do that.

July 5
Mama is doing my portrait and I posed for her for an hour. I like it.

July 6
Mama said she heard Cassie Wallace never was pregnant. I think people say things about Cassie just because she's the kind of person that doesn't care what people think.

July 12
4-H meeting at Pam's house. We spiked the lemonade.

July 13
Angela told me about tampons. She gave me a box and I read the directions in the bathroom and it took me half an hour to figure out how to put one in but I finally did, and now I'm so happy!

July 14
Went swimming and tried to do a backwards flip three times and almost killed myself.

July 16
Plants have feelings. I read it in a science magazine.

July 17
Bad day. Mama made me clean out the refrigerator.

July 18
We leave to go camping tomorrow. Daddy has been studying road maps for weeks. Mama is taking sketchbooks and paints and pencils. Bill wants to fish. I just want to get a good tan.

July 20
Most of New Mexico has no grass and the trees are short as shrubs. The rivers aren't really rivers, they're creeks. We stopped at an adobe church where miracles are supposed to have happened. The

church was extremely old and the floor was off kilter. The altar was hand-carved and painted bright colors. There were about fifteen people wandering in and out, and I knelt and prayed for my family and my friends and our government. To the side of the altar you walked through a doorway into a long narrow room with all different kinds of pictures. There was a paint-by-numbers Jesus. We waited there to go into a small room where only three or four people could fit. The small room had a dirt floor and a big hole and a dipper and people were dipping out handfuls of dirt and putting it in sandwich bags. There was a woman in a wheelchair in line after me. After we came out, I realized that the pictures of people in the room outside were of people who had been healed. I wanted to go back in and get some dirt but Daddy said no.

July 21
Yesterday I wanted to pray for my hair not to be frizzy, but I thought it would be selfish.

July 23
In Colorado it's cold at night, but in the daytime I can sunbathe. I'm having a good time.

July 24
Went rafting on the Snake River. There were three rafts of tourists. In the first raft there was this mother who was the size of a barn and she kept turning around and yelling things at her son who was in my raft and was a shrimp about Bill's age. The water was moving sort of fast, but not too fast, and just as her raft went around a bend, the mother stood up to yell at her son and a branch sticking out over the water knocked her in the river! Then her son stood up and yelled, "Mama, I'll save you!" and jumped in the river! The water was only a couple of feet deep so the guides pulled all the

rafts over on the shore, and everyone sat on the bank for a while. The mother kept hugging her son and saying, "My baby saved my life."

July 26
For sale near the checkout counter at the Hillview Restaurant in Las Vegas, New Mexico: the book *I'm OK—You're OK*, 8-track tape of *Mean as Hell* by Johnny Cash, two kinds of beef jerky, BC powders, several pairs of silver earrings made by real Indians.

July 27
Today the pop-up camper had a flat tire on the highway in the middle of nowhere outside Santa Fe and some men who didn't speak any English tried to help. While they were jacking up the camper, the metal pole they were winding slipped out of someone's hand and swung around and caught Daddy's front shirt pocket and ripped it off! It could have killed him! We're spending the night in Albuquerque. I'm ready to go home.

August 5
No one knows what the school board is going to do. If they don't come up with a desegregation plan, then schools can't open. A monkey at the zoo bit two people from out of town.

August 6
Teaching Vacation Bible School is boring. And there are cartoon pictures of Jesus in the hallway, which seems undignified.

August 7
Wanda has some Tarot cards but I'm afraid of what they will say, so I won't let her do them to me. Saw movie *Live and Let Die*.

August 8
The little kids at Bible school wanted to do the Christmas play and we didn't have a doll for the baby Jesus, so we used a shoe.

August 9
Mama picked me up early from Bible school and when she was backing out of the church parking lot, she scraped the fender of the car next to us. Since no one else was around, she decided to leave a note. She wrote, "I'm so sorry I dented your fender. Please call me at 3 2 3-6 6 8 9." She wrote 9 at the end, instead of another 8, and then she didn't write her name! I said, "Mama, you wrote the wrong number?" and she looked at me like I was a dog that didn't understand people language. Then she put the note on the windshield of the car and we drove home and neither of us said another word.

August 10
Mama changed her mind today about my getting my ears pierced. So I did it. It hurt for about an hour and a half.

August 12
I am 14 years old today. Got perfume and money.

August 13
Pam gave me a box of Tampax for my birthday, which everyone thought was hysterical, but I did not.

August 15
Clothilde told me about a town in Texas called Tree City that's right on the Louisiana border and it was built by this one man, a Jew who made all this money in oil wells and built the city for the people who worked for him, black and white. He gave everyone a piece of

property to live on, and black and white kids played together
& there was none of this stuff like there is in Monroe.

August 16
The school board ruled on a plan to integrate Monroe High with
Lakewood High (which is all black). As of this year, there will be no
sophomores at Monroe High and no freshmen at Lakewood High.
That means all ninth graders in town have to go to Monroe High and
all tenth graders go to Lakewood High. Juniors and seniors can go to
whichever school they choose. Mama says it's drastic.

August 17
Some upset parents had a meeting at Monroe High today. It's because of the sophomore football players having to play for Lakewood for a year and parents thinking that's ruining their lives.
I told Daddy this could be *bad*, and he said, "Don't be silly. People
will get used to it."

August 18
Bought a bow tie at Sears.

August 20
Everyone is worried about desegregation but *my* mother is worried about sex and violence in movies! She's been drawing posters
for the Parents' League that say movies should have warnings for
parents. It's much worse than when she was putting up posters
about fluoride in the city water. Her posters are even in 7-Eleven.
They're *everywhere*.

August 23
Mama dropped me off for my dentist appointment today at the
wrong dentist.

August 24

School board made an amendment to the desegregation plan so kids can play sports for the school that they plan to graduate from. Everyone's happier now.

August 26

E.N. leaves for boarding school soon. Pam doesn't seem too upset.

August 30

First day in high school! My locker is on the third floor. There were hundreds of kids all going in different directions. There's one girl in my homeroom who looks like she swallowed a mattress.

August 31

Pam acted so stuck-up at school today.

September 2

A herd of bees attacked me in the feed room.

September 4

In Tigerette practice after school, it was so hot I almost fainted. Mrs. Glover, the teacher sponsor, stands in the shade and frowns the whole time. When she yells, she sounds like General Patton (or George C. Scott).

September 6

Mother threw away my rock collection. The Junior League was meeting at our house and she cleaned up my room, and she threw away my rock collection without asking! I *hate* leagues. I hate the Parents' League, the Junior League, the Little League, the Charity League. I never even liked the Mickey Mouse Club. Leagues are ruining my life. I am sick to my toenails of Leagues.

September 7
Mama said she threw my rock collection away because it was taking up too much space, and she didn't think it mattered.

September 8
I don't belong in my family.

September 9
Prayed long and hard. Got rid of a lot of self-pride.

September 10
Wore my new boots to school with my jeans tucked in. Pam looked at me funny.

September 11
My favorite class is American History. Coach Baylor is making Eddie Owens wear a tie to school for a week for being rude to him in class. The class is boring but Coach Baylor is interesting.

September 12
I wish I could get a date to the Back-to-School dance, but all the boys ask all the same girls.

September 13
Last night I almost vomited. Finished *Lost Horizon*.

September 14
I was kicked out of the Tigerettes' half-time routine for not having pom-poms and missing practice. Mama wrote me a note that said, "Please excuse Margaret for not having her pom-poms as she couldn't find them." Mrs. Glover read the note and kicked me out of the routine.

September 15

Aunt Lou hasn't gone to work in a week but Angela says she isn't sick. Angela has started walking funny to keep her thighs from touching at the top.

September 16

Saw old Mrs. Parker (who's about eighty years old) riding her lawn mower in her church clothes cutting the grass around her house at about ninety miles an hour.

September 17

Wore my bow tie to school.

October 2

Jim Croce died in a plane crash in Natchitoches on September 20. It's so sad.

October 4

I can't say what's in my head but it's not good.

October 5

Angela says Aunt Lou has gotten to where she won't leave the house and she keeps rearranging the furniture. Angela says she can hear Aunt Lou walking around at night, up and down, up and down. I worry for Angela.

October 7

I don't have a date to Homecoming and it bothers me but I try not to show it.

October 10

A lady at the library told me Daddy saved her life. He took her gall-stones out.

October 11
I feel so unnecessary to the world.

October 12
Coach Baylor passed me a note during class because I was talking. The note said "Miss Sartor, Will You Please Move to the Front of the Room." I had to move by the chalkboard. He made me stay after class to tell me that it's not enough to make good grades—I have to learn to pay attention. I explained that I tended to daydream but would try to do better. He said, "Thank you, Miss Sartor." Coach Baylor is my favorite teacher. No contest.

October 24
Tried to smoke one of Daddy's El Trelles cigars but after two puffs I was ready to El Puke.

October 27
Mama burned the rolls at dinner. Daddy ate them anyway. I have a bad feeling.

October 31
Bill got caught setting off firecrackers in the woods under a toilet seat tied to a tree which black people use when they are fishing back there near the river, and he is grounded for Halloween! My parents can be *mean*.

November 1
If Daddy figures out that I took a cigar from his dresser, I am catfish crap.

November 2
Got a letter from E.N. and wrote him back.

November 3

Aunt Lou came over today and rearranged our living room furniture. When she pulled the green couch away from the wall, she pointed at the back and yelled because there was a map of the neighborhood drawn on the back in RED magic marker! I remembered right away that Tommy and I drew it when we were little and behind the couch was our *Spy Headquarters!* I ran next door to Tommy's house to tell him and we were both *on the floor* laughing. Mama wasn't really that mad. (What could she do?) It was fun talking to Tommy.

November 17

I haven't written in a while but I like this boy named Mitch Hardy and we've had two dates and we're going to the White Rose Ball in December. Our second date was tonight and he kissed me and stuck his tongue in my mouth. I didn't know what to do and I think I acted strange or he acted like I did.

November 18

Sticking your tongue in someone's mouth is called Frenching and Wanda thinks it's great.

November 19

Mitch acted funny at school today.

November 25

Mitch didn't ask me out for this weekend.

November 26

Mitch completely ignores me in front of other girls.

December 2

Mitch had a date with Hallie last night but it doesn't bother me.

December 4
Hallie is a big flirt-butt and I think everyone is starting to hate her.

December 8
A policeman pulled Mama over today but he didn't give her a ticket because Daddy is his doctor. Mama told him she didn't know it was illegal to drive over a firehose.

December 10
Daddy took Bill deer hunting because Bill wanted to go. (I've never known Daddy to go hunting before.) Bill told me they sat in a deer stand in the freezing cold for over an hour. Then some deer walked out in the clearing and Daddy pointed and said that one is a little spike, and Bill shot it and the rest ran away. Then the fawns walked out of the woods crying for their mothers who had run off, so Daddy made Bill wait until the mother deer came back and got the babies. Then Daddy and Bill dragged the dead deer to the truck, where some other men slit it open and wiped the blood on Bill's face. Bill said he felt guilty when he heard the fawns crying. Now the dead deer is strung up on our swingset.

December 14
E.N. is home from boarding school & he came over & we talked. Mostly he wanted to talk about Pam.

December 20
Ernest the yardman brought Stella a Christmas present. It was a box of "Evening In Paris" cologne (with powder and a puff) & Daddy told Stella to tell Ernest she was getting married (even though she isn't) and she did. Ernest said he was happy for her and that he thought about her all the time and he hoped she would

be happy. Stella made me sit in the room with them. I pretended to
be reading a book.

December 22
I had a shitty time tonight at the White Rose Ball. Mitch barely
talked to me and we spent most of the night watching Tony get his
car unstuck from the mud. The best part was that no one vomited
on me.

December 25
I got my own stereo and I am sooooo haaaaappy!!! Tommy came
over and brought his Barbra Streisand records and we had a fantastic time talking about my horrible date last weekend. Went over
to Momma Doll's for Christmas dinner.

December 28
E.N. came over and we listened to Don McLean's *American Pie* over
and over and tried to figure out what all the lyrics meant. E.N. said
I was Miss American Pie. I think he was stoned.

December 29
I am not getting along with Mama. Not with Daddy either for that
matter.

December 30
Mitch asked me out for New Year's Eve. It makes no sense.

December 31
Had fun tonight with Mitch but something bothers me. I get the
feeling he likes me but he wishes he didn't.

1974

"I wonder if Jesus was sexy."

January 1
Stayed in my room.

January 2
Been hanging out with E.N., but only as a friend. He calls me Margaret Earline and I call him Edgar Napoleon.

January 5
Margaret sounds like a boring old lady. The only Margaret I know is the one in *Dennis the Menace* and she's a prickette. Mama says there is a princess in England named Margaret, but who knows that? I've decided to go by my middle name—*Earline*.

January 6
Daddy took Stella back to New Orleans and Momma Doll and I went along. We stayed two nights in a hotel in the French Quarter. On the way back, Momma Doll kept saying, "Tom, you got to let me pay my share." Daddy said over and over, "No, Mrs. Lawton, you're my mother-in-law and it's my treat." But she kept asking, so finally he said, "Well, I guess it came to about five hundred dollars." Momma Doll got real quiet and after a minute she said, "Well, golly wop." And then she didn't mention it again.

January 7
Riding today, I saw a kingfisher sitting in a dead tree by the river. I watched until it flew away because I've never seen one before.

January 8
Why does it scare me to think I might be ordinary? I remember when I started first grade and I could hardly pay attention for fear I wouldn't learn how to read and write. I didn't want to be like

everyone else. I didn't want to have to learn. I wanted to know everything already.

January 10
No one even TRIES to remember to call me Earline. Daddy suggested Peggy, but there is no way I'm going to be Peggy.

January 13
The way Mitch treats me is bad for me. E.N. has gone back to boarding school.

January 14
Finished *A Tale of Two Cities.*

January 22
Got a letter from E.N. and at the end he wrote, "Well, you can write me if you want to."

January 30
I'm so attracted to Mitch & I wish I could make it stop.

February 1
Aunt Lou does really nice things when she feels good (like cook food for sick people) but when she feels bad, she doesn't want to see anybody.

February 5
Got braces on top teeth. Now my entire mouth is full of metal. When I saw Tommy in the driveway, he covered his eyes. He said he couldn't see because the sun was reflecting off my mouth.

February 11
Vernon asked me to the Heart Fund dance. This is very good.

February 16
Vernon was nice but he can't dance. I danced some with a junior named Chris who was going wild and *that* was fun.

February 19
Went out drinking with Tommy and Pam for something to do.

February 23
Nothing happening.

February 24
I feel bad.

February 25
Reading *The Exorcist.*

February 26
I was reading in the kitchen with my feet propped up on the table and Tommy walked in the back door. He was in a serious mood and said, "We're having this meeting at our house tonight. It's part of a witness mission at our church and I want you to come. I think it'll be pretty neat." I didn't have anything else to do so I went.

There were a lot of cars in the driveway and out in the street. It was a big meeting. Inside everyone was sitting on furniture or on the floor and there was a guy in the middle with a guitar (Roody). Everyone was singing and clapping and some were even crying. I saw Tommy in the corner singing away. The whole thing was weird but nice. When the singing was over, the guy with the guitar started talking about Jesus Christ as his best friend and how Christ brings us together and then he asked people from the group to talk about what had happened to them and they did. (I didn't understand what it was all about.) This boy named Jackson started talking. (Jackson is this tall, crazy jock from Monroe High who is known to drink like a fish and date lots of girls and I know him but I've never hardly said hello to him.) He was sitting in a blue director's chair to the side of the room and said, "I've never felt this great in my entire life." Then he started crying! I was staring moon-eyed. I looked around and everyone in the room was just as emotional. Huge tears started coming down my face. After the meeting, I walked out in the driveway with Tommy & a girl I didn't know came up and hugged Tommy around his neck. What I'm feeling makes no sense to me.

February 27
I *felt* the love in that room last night and I *want* it. When I talked to Tommy, he said he wanted to get to know me better. That made me happy.

(later)
I'm searching but I'm afraid I'm not as sincere as I should be.

February 28
I rode in the woods and when I talked to Rex he nodded his head like he understood.

March 1
I went to another prayer meeting with Tommy. There were a lot of college students and people I didn't know there. Everyone was so happy. (I don't mean pleasant—I mean ear-to-ear *happy!*) It was an old house on a corner with a screen porch. Inside there

were probably 3o people. We sat in as much of a circle as was possible but it was crowded. First we sang all kinds of songs, very simple ones that just blended into one another without a break. Then a boy stood up and started talking about the spirit of Christ Jesus. I didn't understand what he meant by "spirit" but he explained about how in the Bible it tells that the spirit of Jesus came back to live in the hearts of men after his crucifixion. Later, a girl in her twenties by the name of Andrea took me into a separate room and she sat down and held my hands, palm on palm, between us.

"Margaret, how do you feel?"

"Wonderful . . . I guess."

"Do you know how very beautiful it is to be a Christian? To be a loved child of God? To make Jesus your best friend?"

"Not really."

"Do you want to?"

"I think so."

Inside I was groping—and then I felt like suddenly the confines in which I'd existed all my fourteen years were too *small* and I wanted to bust open! After praying, we returned to the main room where everyone was in a circle with their arms around one another, heads bowed, praying. One of the leaders said, "Does anyone wish us to lay our hands on them and pray for them?" He explained where in the Bible, Jesus had instructed the "laying on of hands" & that we should pray for one another's needs. I felt a *tremendous need* to be prayed for but I wasn't sure what for. Other people entered the middle of the circle and people prayed (some of them were praying in some language that wasn't English). I entered the circle and someone asked what I needed to be prayed for. I said I wasn't sure. Then I closed my eyes and felt hands touching my head, my shoulders, my sides and my back, and I heard one voice say, "This girl has decided to give her life to you, not in slavery, but in freedom." I heard murmuring all around like, "Yes, Lord" and "Thank you, Jesus" and inside I was churning—a feeling beyond explanation, like nothing I have ever felt before, and it was God.

Someone said, "Pray, Margaret. Pray out loud. Pray in a heavenly language if you want to. Do you want to?" (I thought—Me?) "Say, Abba, Margaret. It means father in Hebrew." And then, I did. I just let the words come, let them flow, and it didn't need to be explained to me because I could hardly restrain it—my spirit was in control. I began to let the words flow, and the words weren't mine, they were words I didn't know, had never heard—they were being spoken by me! I could control the speed and tone of my voice, but the words were not coming from my mind. It was such a release!! I felt I was talking face to face with God Almighty himself! I moved back into the circle of people, tears pouring down my face. Tommy put his arms around me. He was crying too. It seemed *everyone* was crying.

On the way home Tommy told me the same thing had happened to him two days ago but he hadn't told me because he was afraid I might not come to the meetings. He said we have been "born again."

There is sense of peace in me right now BUT I can't deny the doubts I have—the temptations the Devil is *already putting in my mind.* SO I keep praying to help me believe this is *real.*

March 2

I'm feeling so HIGH. Chris (the junior I danced with at the Heart Fund dance) called me tonight. I think my prayers are being answered.

March 3

My life is changing.

March 5
Talked to Tommy's older sister, who was born again a while ago, and she said committing your life to Jesus is no small matter, and can't be understood, but that we must learn that there is both good and evil, and God is good and the devil is evil. She says now that we have decided to live our lives for Christ, the devil will do everything he can to get us back. (I could already tell.)

March 6
Chris has been flirting with me.

March 8
God is so powerful & capable of anything! (But I must remember to take him seriously.)

March 9
I'm just a baby Christian and because of that Satan is putting all kinds of thoughts in my head to talk me out of what I believe.

March 10
At prayer meetings, I feel so much more *alive*.

March 12
I healed myself yesterday.

March 13
Chris gave me a ride home after the Monroe High talent show tonight and he took me parking. I wasn't sure if I should but we did. We have a date Saturday night.

March 14
Today at school I felt separate from Jesus.

March 15

Chris and I went to a movie and he kissed me good night at the front door. When I got inside, Mama came storming down the hall saying, "What do you think you were doing out there?"—Mama *watched* me kiss Chris good night through the window in Bill's room! I am SO MAD. I didn't do *anything* wrong!

March 16

The prayer meeting was at the Parkers' big house and we performed small miracles. We prayed and grew everyone's two legs to be the same length. (It's a fact that 98% of people have one leg shorter than the other.) A boy named Julius was there and praying in tongues and then he started laughing very strangely. Mrs. Parker and her oldest son Ellis took him away to another room and Ellis told us a false spirit had entered Julius and the elders would pray for him. I left at 12:30 a.m. and they were still in another part of the house and hadn't finished. Mama was upset but fairly calm when I came in so late. We had a long talk about the prayer meetings but I didn't tell her about Julius.

March 17

Went to church with Chris & then over to his house. I felt funny though because Chris tried to kiss me when we were alone and I didn't think it was right to do that in his parents' house.

March 20

Chris hasn't talked to me much at school this week.

March 24

English and Algebra tests both easy.

March 25

Big argument with Mama. She made all these new rules, like it doesn't *count* as being home from a date until I'm inside the house and Chris is gone. I don't think my parents like Chris.

March 26

I have no security except Jesus.

March 27

After dinner, I asked Mama if she believed in God. She said she wished she could say yes, but she couldn't. I told her I believed in God, and she said that was probably a good thing for me. Then I said, "But *why* don't you believe in God?" And she said, "I don't know, Margaret. It's just one of those things." Then she went in her studio to paint.

March 28

Mama & Daddy don't realize how Jesus is making my life so much more *real*.

March 29

People at school talk behind our backs and call us Jesus freaks, but I'm not going to let it bother me because my eternal life is at stake.

March 30

Aunt Lou took too many pills and my uncle found her unconscious and called Daddy and they took her to the hospital. They pumped her stomach and now she is OK. Mama is upset though and Angela won't talk about it. Momma Doll doesn't know and I heard Mama say to Daddy that she might not tell her. I don't know what to do.

March 31

Aunt Lou has to go to a mental hospital because it's the law. Mama says it's good that she has to go because otherwise Aunt Lou wouldn't get any help. Mama lied to Momma Doll and said that Aunt Lou had up and decided to visit Robert and his wife and didn't want to talk to anyone until she got back. (Mama can *lie* like it is *nobody's business.*)

April 1

I hear God telling me not to worry but I don't know what's happening with me.

April 2

Mama says Aunt Lou hates the hospital and wants to come home. I don't understand why God let this happen.

April 3

My prayer group is praying for Aunt Lou to be healed. Tommy is getting to be good friends with Jackson Bishop.

April 4

Daddy is worried because he said a doctor he knows who goes to prayer meetings has started praying over patients. He sat me down and told me not to believe in miracles & such. He said being a Christian is fine, but that God heals through good doctors.

April 6

Jackson was in a four-car wreck & not hurt. It was a miracle.

April 7

Mama says Stella is having a hard time at college so I'm praying for her.

April 8

Tommy calls me Maggie. No one in my whole life has ever called me Maggie and I like it, which says something.

April 9

Chris told me he loved me. I didn't know what to say, so I said thank you.

April 10

Chris called me while I was at Angela's house. He said he had to tell me something. I couldn't talk though & I didn't want to leave, so he didn't get to.

April 11

Chris and I had a big fight! He found out that I told Tommy that he told me he loved me. I was mad but I learned something. I learned that I shouldn't tell things to people if there is a chance I might regret it later.

April 12

Tommy woke me up this morning and I was in bed with snot in my eyes and he said I looked pretty! I was so embarrassed. So I went in the bathroom and brushed my hair up over my head so it stuck out like wire and I walked back in my room with my hands pressed against my sides and said, "I am zee human Q-tip." We both fell out laughing. We just fell out.

April 13

I was home alone & Chris came over and we started watching TV. When Mama came home she made Chris leave. I could tell she was mad. When Daddy got home, he told me to tell Chris to come over tomorrow after church & he said, "You tell him to wear a jacket and tie."

April 14

Chris came over. He wore his jacket, but not a tie. I was listening from the kitchen and Chris tried to explain, but before he could, Daddy said, "If I ever catch you at my house alone with my daughter again, I'll *shoot* you."

April 15

The doctors are letting Aunt Lou come home from the hospital and Mama thinks Aunt Lou fooled them. Everyone is a little upset around here.

April 16

Mama thinks I'm seeing too much of Chris. I told Chris what she said. He says he loves me.

April 17

I think I've decided to like (love?) Chris.

April 18

Daddy thinks fourteen is too young to go steady. He says I will meet lots of boys and I have to do what he says. I asked him what he would say if I had a date with a black boy and he answered that I could go out with *any* boy as long as the boy was polite and showed up at the front door and had taken a bath. I just don't see how parents think they have the right to tell you what to do.

April 19

So many things told me that something was wrong with Chris tonight. Finally he said that he had forgotten God because he was afraid of losing me. Now I *know* I love him.

April 20
Chris & I have so much *affection* for one another & I think it must be because of Jesus.

April 21
Chris got a speeding ticket & lost his temper. I read him a Bible verse and he calmed down.

April 22
I've been asking God to tell me what to do about Mitch because Mitch has been flirting with me. I think God told me. I think I'm supposed to bring Mitch to God. That's why Jesus took my feelings for Mitch & gave them to Chris. So I don't think it's wrong for me to talk to Mitch.

April 23
Angela has this little book with the calories of everything in it. She adds up the calories she eats and then figures out how long she has to exercise to burn them off. It's driving me bananas.

April 24
Went skiing on the bayou. Mitch kept flirting with me and I kept liking it.

April 25
Sometimes I have thoughts that I shouldn't and God is helping me learn not to.

April 26
I know I am an orphan in my dream. I am in a room with other girls and we are sitting in a circle on the floor. There is a package

behind me—it's a mailer (padded) and I've had it with me all my life, but no one has ever looked inside of it. There's a knock and two men are coming after me and they want the package. A boy comes in and he is an orphan too and he understands and helps me escape. We are on a bridge and I plead with an old woman to let me borrow her pony. "It's a life-or-death matter," I say, and she gives me the pony, & the boy and I get on the pony and start running. We are trying to get home.

April 27
Saw Tex Roper walking across the Ouachita River bridge today. Tex is this man who walks around town dressed like a cowboy, carrying bridles & stuff, and Daddy gives him rides. Once I saw his house. It's surrounded with a chain link fence that has saddles and stirrups and halters hanging all over it. Tex is a World War II veteran like Daddy.

April 28
Every time I see Mitch I like it, and so I guess I like him. I talked to Chris about splitting up but he kept saying how much he loved me & so we're still dating.

April 29
My feelings are all mixed up. Tommy tapped at my window around 11 p.m. and we sat in my kitchen & ate leftovers. It's so easy for me to talk to Tommy. I told him that I want him to be my next door neighbor *forever.* He said I might have to move to New York because that's where he planned to live, and be an artist, and have fabulous dinner parties. I said, "What if I'm not fabulous?" He said, "Maggie, you're not fabulous *yet,* because you live in a stinky little town where all the girls wear too much makeup."

April 30
I finally realized through Tommy and the grace of God that I had to break it off with Chris. I did and I was so *filled* with the glory of God! I felt so *happy* that I knew it was God's will! I only pray that Chris eventually receives the *joy* from this that I have.

May 1
Chris called and apologized for the things he said to me last night.

May 2
We had a prayer meeting down by the bayou. It was very peaceful. I've never written this before, but I think I'm going to fall in love with Jackson Bishop—not now but later.

May 3
Skipped fifth period at school. It was too *hot* to be in school. I walked over to the bayou and went swimming in my underwear.

May 4
Went to a concert with Chris. (We'd planned to go before I broke up.) He didn't say two words to me the whole time and then in the car he kissed me & said he couldn't help it because he loved me and I started crying. The music was great though.

May 5
Hung out with Tommy and Jackson. I felt *so* attracted to Jackson . . . but in a *different* way.

May 6
Liking Jackson is a BAD idea.

May 7

Tommy says Jackson is the best thing that ever happened to him. He called Jackson his *savior* because he used to avoid the jocks at school, but now he can walk right by them and they don't say anything, just because he's Jackson's friend.

May 8

Pam told me how to give a hickie (you suck) and tried to give me one on my leg but I wouldn't let her. Wanda said she *always* French kisses—one time for nine minutes!

May 9

I have a date with Mitch tomorrow night! Chris called so I told him, and he hung up on me. I'm still praying my feelings for Jackson will go away.

May 10

Chris skipped school today so I didn't see him. I felt so UP all day. Had a GREAT date with Mitch. Aunt Lou called and told Mama that she woke up this morning and the dark clouds had gone away!

May 11

Chris asked me to go out with him just to talk so I did, but he wouldn't talk and he expected me to make out with him. I wouldn't & he got pissed. We talked & I let him & then he wouldn't get off me.

May 12

We got our annuals today and I am the only girl in the entire annual that has her hair in braids. The only girl who looks worse is

Beth Bilberry, who parts her afro in the middle and looks like she's wearing Mickey Mouse ears.

May 13
Pam said the Lord told Wanda she was going to die soon.

May 15
My old life is breaking away.

May 16
The Lord told me to talk to Wanda.

May 18
Wanda told me that her family life is a wreck & she is *so* unhappy. I have to remember how *small* my problems are & that I have to help others if I expect to be helped. I decided that I don't like Mitch anymore & I feel free & happy.

May 20
I feel really bad.

May 21
I'm going to join Tommy's church youth group for the summer because they have a new youth director named Doug Reed. He goes to seminary. He is very thin with hair down to his shoulders and he reminds me of Jesus.

May 22
Tommy accused me of joining his church's youth group just because Doug Reed is cute. I told him that I would *never* make a decision about my spiritual life based on something so superficial. He said, "Maggie, we are *so alike* in that way."

May 23

Mitch had a date with Hallie Saturday night. It doesn't hurt me at all. I did hear a rumor that the football players call her "Hot Hallie" but I doubt it's true.

May 25

Jackson asked to go riding on Rex with me. That was a surprise.

May 26

I don't know if my physical desires are normal or sinful, but they are certainly distracting.

May 28

". . . Let us lay aside every weight and the sin which doth so easily beset us. And let us run with patience the race that is set before us . . ." (Hebrews 12:1)

May 29

I have been praying to Jesus and the Holy Ghost for *patience* and I have also mentioned that it would help if I did not have frizzy hair.

June 1

My life is so much better (than it was) so why don't I feel good?

June 2

Tommy is going to summer school in Georgia, which *sucks* . . . but E.N. is coming home from boarding school soon, which is *grooooovy.*

June 3

Wanda asked me if I was worried about Angela but I wasn't sure what she was talking about.

June 5
Went for a walk on the levee with Mitch. He kissed me & I asked him to the Sadie Hawkins dance.

June 7
I can't stop thinking about Mitch.

June 8
At the dance, Mitch had his eye on Alice the whole time. Chris was drunk and with a girl who just moved here that I don't know and was dancing like a tornado.

June 9
Today Chris had hickies all over his neck and he was *showing them off*. He's really sick.

June 10
I'm praying about my anxiety. Losing Mitch to another girl doesn't hurt *too* much. It's just that I feel like I really *need* him.

June 11
Started period. Went to Assembly of God revival & people were being healed & slain in the Spirit. Seeing them made me so emotional that I forgot all my worries & prayed for them. I know God is going to make my life happy one day. Whatever Mitch does can't hurt me because I love Jesus. *Satan is working on me though.*

June 12
I'm confused about how my life will turn out.

June 13
Mama FORGOT to pick me up from summer school and I had to walk home. I've decided to never speak to her again.

June 14

Saw Diana Portman crying hard today. She said her parents won't let her date John Rowan anymore because they think it's grown too serious and he's not Jewish. I've never heard of such of thing.

June 15

I miss Tommy. Mama's apologized. Daddy is teaching me how to drive.

June 16

Mama told me Mrs. Portman was in a concentration camp during the war and that's why she doesn't want her daughter dating boys who aren't Jewish. Mama told me that Daddy had a girlfriend once (before her) who was Catholic, and to Daddy's mother, being Catholic was like being from a different race, so they had to break up. Daddy having a girlfriend besides Mama is hard to imagine.

June 17

I've got to start thinking of other people's happiness before my own. I gave Daddy a Father's Day card and I think it touched him, or it seemed like it did.

June 18

A boy I met at Wanda's called me four times and it's creepy because he's a worm.

June 19

Mitch told Edgar Napoleon that he wanted to date me, but that he was afraid people would talk about him because I go to prayer meetings. I told E.N. that maybe I'm not meant to date someone— I may not have the personality for it. Unfortunately, he agreed.

June 20

Sometimes I get this deep *aching* for romantic companionship, but then sometimes I feel so peaceful being free.

June 21

Maybe I should become a nun.

June 22

Read up on nuns and I think I'd make a better veterinarian.

June 23

When Julius and Doug Reed argue at youth group over the right and wrong way to worship God, I can't stand it! Right now God is my *entire* existence. And Julius is completely off his nuts.

June 24

Wanda is turning weird. She quit wearing a bra & doesn't shave her legs.

June 25

O code for completely depressed.

June 26

Doug Reed has all the kids fixing up a cinder-block storage shed at the back of the church property. We're painting the inside beige and brown and putting down orange indoor-outdoor carpet. It's going to be our youth hut.

June 27

Some of my friends went to the Country Club to swim but Daddy told me to quit going there so I came home. E.N. told me someone called Mitch a Jesus freak because of me. Because I'm a freak.

June 28
C Feeling mediocre (not happy or sad) and trying not to.

June 29
Boring day.

June 30
Daddy told me his mother decided before she died exactly what she wanted carved on her headstone. So it says, "I have fought the good fight. I have followed my course. I have kept the faith." (God, I wish I had known her.)

July 1
Bought *For The Roses* by Joni Mitchell.

July 2
O I know I should just be happy and accept things as they are but I can't.

July 3
O *For The Roses* is not great. Or maybe it's just me.

July 4
Tommy is HOME!!! (Only for a couple of days.) Ate and ate and ate forever.

July 5
Tommy and I stole a six-pack of beer from Buddy Regal's truck and we drank it behind the levee and had so much fun until I threw up. Good night.

July 6

Today I rode my bike over to the city courts where Mrs. Portman was playing tennis with Mama. Mrs. Portman has red hair and a loud voice and speaks with a thick German accent. When she came off the court for water, she reached for a cup from the stack right next to me and that was when I noticed the numbers tattooed on her wrist. When she walked back on the court, I left. The whole ride home my eyes stung and my nose and jaw felt like they were being pinched. I keep thinking how there is *so much* I don't know, and *no one is letting on.*

July 7

There was a family supper at our church tonight & Mitch was there & asked if he could give me a ride home. I have to admit how good it felt to be with him, and it makes me realize how I need that *kind* of love. Still, I can't change just to suit him. Because dying of meaninglessness would be worse than dying of loneliness.

July 8

Last night I prayed and prayed that the burden of human desire be taken from me.

July 9

Jackson came by & brought a baby kitten he had found. We bought her some food and named her Ruth. The flat-out truth is that Jackson is getting under my skin. I don't think there's a chance he would like me but he does seem to pay attention to me.

July 10

I'm confused as to whether my need of the flesh is against my ful-fillment of the spirit. Are sexual desires bad for me? I know it's not sinful like adultery or uncleanliness or idolatry, but it is a powerful need. I keep thinking God promises peace, love, and joy, but he also promises *long suffering*. The part about long suffering confuses me, because peace & suffering do not seem to go hand in hand.

July 11

I'm very thin. Daddy x-rayed me, but didn't find anything. He says I'm growing fast and need to eat more, but the real problem is that my body needs things that I don't want it to need and when I try to stop the other feelings, my hunger goes away too.

July 12

"For every man shall bear his own burden." (Galatians 6:5) I will always be in need of some kind of *boy–girl* relationship. My need for love *from* people, as well as *for* people, is something that must be fulfilled for me to be happy. I guess that's my burden.

July 13

I haven't told anyone about my feelings for Jackson, but they're just getting stronger and there's no getting around it.

July 14

We had prayer meeting at the youth hut tonight. It was pouring rain outside with cracks of lightning and booming thunder. We started hearing sirens so we gathered at the door and were watching the police cars and fire engines beginning to arrive. Then, at the same time, all of us noticed the bright orange fire high up on the steeple of the church. When Doug Reed saw it, he said, "Shit, it's the church!" and he was halfway across the field in a dead run before anyone else had regained their senses. By the time all of us were over there, the fire engines were hooked up and ready to go. Doug got us all inside taking cushions & books off the first pews and covering them with canvas. It was really exciting! Later we had a water balloon fight!

July 15
This feeling for Jackson doesn't depress or worry or nag at me, but it's always there, a kind of wishful closeness.

July 16
Daddy got me up at 6 a.m. to go to surgery with him. We had breakfast in the hospital cafeteria. We scrubbed together and I stood right next to the head of the patient, where I had a good view. Uncle Henry was on one side and Daddy on the other. Since Daddy is left-handed and Uncle Henry is right-handed and they both wear wire-rimmed glasses, they looked like mirror images. When Daddy made the first cut I got dizzy and had to go lie down on a gurney in the hallway until I felt better. Then I went back in and watched for over an hour. The anesthesiologist made jokes about the woman's tits.

July 18
Jackson and I rode Rex double today. Rex didn't mind and we didn't talk much. We saw a pileated woodpecker in a tree and followed it, which wasn't easy. We followed it for more than an hour, to a dead tree on a steep cutaway bank of the river. We saw it go into a hole in the tree—completely go in. When it came out and flew away, we heard the racket of baby birds. I was so excited!

July 19
Signed up for cheerleader tryouts, which is a stupid idea. But Angela wants to do it and I want to be with Angela.

July 20
It worries me that my feelings for Jackson could be a bad thing for my friendship with Tommy.

July 21

Doug Reed organized a lock-in sleepover at the church. We had pizza and played hide-and-go-seek in the building with all the lights off. We slept in the sanctuary in sleeping bags. It was a blast!

July 22

Practiced cheers with Angela. We talked about how we felt about boys trying stuff with us. Angela won't let her boyfriend do anything. I'm no good in these conversations because I don't *know* what I think. And Chris doesn't count.

July 23

Every once in a while, at prayer meeting, the way people talk makes me uncomfortable and I start to feel like I'm locked in a cage being poked at.

July 24

I think my depressions come when I let myself worry over superficial things and so I've decided to release myself from these worries and expand my knowledge of God.

July 25

O Went to a YMCA dance tonight and Chris was there. I have this deep resentment of Chris. He makes me feel dirty and so I hate myself. I don't know how to stop these feelings and for some reason I'm afraid to pray to God to take them away. Tony showed me his new orange Cutlass, and that was good because orange is my good-luck color.

July 26

There was a competition at the cheerleader tryout clinic and my group got a blue ribbon. Pam's group got a red ribbon & I know it killed her.

July 27
The prayer group has dwindled considerably.

July 30
BIG argument at prayer meeting! Doug Reed said that it's "un-healthy shit" to think that Christians won't have differences of opinions. Then Julius accused Doug of being "sent by the enemy." I walked out & sat on the grass in front of the dentist's office across the street until Betsy drove me home.

August 1
Doug Reed is naturally sexy, which I think could be a problem for a minister. I wonder if Jesus was sexy?

August 2
Everyone is out of town.

August 3
A kid from Ouachita High shot himself.

August 4
I think if you are so unhappy that dying seems better than living, then God would understand if you wanted to die.

August 5
Saw E.N. and I was hurt because he didn't speak to me, but he has a new girlfriend, Arabella, who gets very jealous.

August 6
Boy–girl desires *haunt* me, but less than they did.

August 7
In my dream this woman wanted to show me her pregnant mares and so I followed her into the pasture and we were standing there when she looked back & saw the gate was open. I had left the gate open! Some of the mares had gotten loose. We chased after them but one of them ran out into the street and slipped on the pavement and fell and died.

August 8
President Nixon resigned. Made appointment to get my hair cut.

August 9
Got my hair cut. It was rainy today so it frizzed, but I'm satisfied.

August 10
Tommy is home! We talked & talked & I'm sooooo happy to see him.

August 11
At 6 a.m., I snuck into Tommy's house and woke him up & then we drove over and got Jackson and we all had breakfast at the Holiday Grill. I was so happy!! I was almost in tears I was so happy.

August 12
Fifteen years old today! All my friends gave me presents. Later, I went for a walk and asked God about why I need my friends so much, but he didn't tell me why.

August 13
Rode Rex way back in the swampy woods. On the way back, I was riding on top of the levee and a buck with a big rack of antlers ran

out of the woods on one side of the levee and disappeared into the woods on the other side. It gave me a very bad feeling.

August 14
I don't exactly feel lost, it's more like I feel *misplaced.* I must belong *somewhere,* but I don't think I belong here.

August 15
The new haircut is a problem.

August 17
Parting hair off-center with bangs now.

August 18
Prayer meetings aren't feeling so lively since Doug Reed left to go back to seminary.

August 20
I've gained weight. (Unfortunately, it's not in my boobs.)

August 25
I want a date to the Back-to-School dance but it doesn't matter too much.

August 26
Got my driver's license. I passed the written part but almost failed the driving.

August 27
Trying not to think about the dance but it's the idea of no one wanting me that hurts.

August 28
Start school at Lakewood High tomorrow.

August 29
First day at Lakewood. Newspaper photographers were there taking photos of the white kids stepping off the bus. School's gonna be OK. Lakewood's really clean.

August 30
I got some good classes, but the only boy in them is Mitch, which is bad.

September 3
Mitch & I get along fine, but in class I catch him watching me & it drives me crazy.

September 4
Sometimes when you're peeing and you stop pushing the pee out, you can hear the pee hitting the water so you know you're still peeing but you don't feel anything coming out of your body and it's strange. Another thought: I think it would great to be able to pee standing up and without pulling your pants down to your knees.

September 5
I felt fine at school but there was a poster party tonight and Mitch *snobbed* me right in front of Bonnie Dell, who is a new girl he's been dating. The Guess Who was playing over some outdoor speakers and I went & sat in the dark under a bush and watched people drinking & yelling & it pulled me apart inside.

September 6
Honey got in the kitchen and knocked over the birdcage and *ate* Bandito.

September 7
If me & Tommy are in the middle of a conversation in his room and one of us has to pee, we don't even close the bathroom door all the way, and we keep talking. And Mama doesn't care if Tommy comes in my room and wakes me up in the morning. Sometimes I feel like Tommy is my brother and other times I feel like we're practically married.

September 11
Practiced cheerleading (for tryouts tomorrow) until 6:30 p.m. & then all the girls who are trying out sat around outside the gym and talked. It made me kind of sick to my stomach to see how nervous everyone was.

September 12
I didn't make cheerleader. Neither did Angela or Pam. Mitch's new girlfriend Bonnie Dell did. (Dell is her last name, but no one calls her just Bonnie, everyone says Bonnie Dell.)

September 13
Saw E.N. and he looked sick. (stoned?)

September 15
I've really been getting down about never having a date. The plain rotten truth is that no one wants me. It bothers me that I'm jealous of Bonnie Dell and that's she's beautiful and that I might hate her.

September 16
I like Bonnie Dell. She's nice. It's not her fault her legs look like tree trunks.

September 17
The jealousy over Mitch is slipping away & I pray that it will go away because I can't tell whether it actually is, or I'm just trying to convince myself that it is.

September 18
I wish I could wake up in the morning and feel no jealousy at all. And I would like to be a boy. I would be a much cuter boy.

September 19
I'm lonely . . . a tiny dancer . . . mad girl across the water. Today at lunch Angela ate three peas and a cracker and said she was *full.*

September 20
After the football game, I went with Pam and hung out in the parking lot behind the 7-Eleven. Everyone was drinking and the boys were only talking to certain girls and I had a *lousy* time.

September 21
God loves a cheerful giver. I've decided to be cheerful.

September 22
Cheerfulness is not in my nature. I've decided I'm going to improve my mind instead. I'm also considering giving away all my favorite clothes.

September 23

God has been sending me messages & I think He's saying, "You can be a better person than this." I hear it, but I don't think it's working.

September 24

Angela has a boyfriend and I'd like to be more happy for her but I'm too selfish.

September 25

I mix up my M's and N's and my P's and B's and swish my spit and say one word when I mean another word and it's so fucking frustrating! I need a tongue transplant.

September 26

"What a Friend We Have in Jesus" is a ridiculous song in my opinion.

September 27

The Monroe High football game tonight was in Bastrop and we beat the hell out of them—but afterward, there was some yelling going on from Bastrop kids standing around the Tigerette buses and some Tigerettes were yelling back. Then as the buses pulled out, a rock crashed through the window of my bus like a missile, and it barely missed a girl's face and hit someone's arm. *All the buses stopped.* Mrs. Glover climbed up the steps of every bus full of crying hysterical girls, and told us to keep our heads down until we were out of town. We were terrified! I got dizzy with my head down and tried to keep my eyes closed because the bus was bumping over tire ruts and I thought I was going to throw up. When we finally got to smooth road, I started talking nonstop to Angela, who was next to me, but she kept her eyes shut and hissed at me to be quiet. Across the aisle, Pam kept popping up her head and laughing.

September 29
I'm afraid of the sadness in me.

September 30
At prayer meeting, this blind girl Molly & her husband talked to us & there was something so pure about them. She did most of the talking, but kept reaching over and touching him, and he kept his eyes on her. I was so moved. For some people, I think love is like a secret between them.

October 1
Angela wants us to start doing more things together.

October 2
I can't describe what's going on in my head, but it's good. Today Angela said I was her best friend. I *love* Angela. It's scary how much I love her.

October 3
Everyone I know has a date to the Homecoming dance. I *know* my friends feel sorry for me and I can't stand that! I've decided to pray for a date.

October 4
Jackson and I rode Rex for hours back in Chauvin woods, and Jackson got carried away and started making up poems, reciting out loud, "O, tree, O tree, what have you seen?"—that kind of thing. Then we glanced around and just a few feet away from us was a hunter. He was standing there in his hunting clothes, rifle in

his hand and with a totally amazed and slightly angry look on his face. I guess he wasn't too happy about the poetry reading! I said to Jackson, "Hold on!" and he grabbed my waist and I wheeled Rex around and we bolted away. Jackson was so embarrassed—but I thought it was hilarious!

October 7
The Homecoming dance is this weekend & I still don't have a date. I've prayed about it. I know it wouldn't hurt me to have a date, and it would surely improve my mood.

October 8
I have a DATE with Tony! Hallelujah!!!!!!!!!!

October 9
Tommy told me that Jackson is *upset* that someone else asked me to the dance? I asked him *why*, and he said it was probably because I ran into his house wiggling my ass and yelling "Praise the Lord." I told him, "But I was *happy* . . . I only wiggle when I'm *happy!*"And Tommy said, "I just think Jackson is confused about you, Margaret."

October 11
I had a fun date! Before the dance, I was a little worried that Tony would take me parking and want to make out and he did, twice, but both times I prayed & God brought me through it.

October 12
I woke up before dawn and couldn't go back to sleep, so I got dressed and walked outside. I grabbed the halter from the tack room and walked towards the levee. From the top of the levee, I could see Rex in the middle of the pen, sleeping lying down. By the

time I got to the gate, his head was up and he had straightened his front legs. Then as I walked in the pen, he swung his neck and head sideways and forward. He *lurched* and hoisted himself up. I was there with the lead rope around his neck just as he made it to his feet. He stretched out his neck, twitched his muscles, and shook his head—the shake moving all the way down his body to his tail. Then he exhaled, making a very loud noise. By then the sun was just coming up over the trees and I went riding.

October 13
There is a problem. My attraction to Jackson bothers me. But I also have this strange certainty that I *love* him.

October 14
I feel trapped by my own self. I can't get away from me.

October 16
I've skipped a bunch of classes this week. I skipped for three hours today. But I can pull out the tests, so what does it matter? What's BOTHERING me is that Jackson's girlfriend Jane (the cheerleader from Shreveport) is coming into town this weekend . . . and the point is that I don't know why I let myself get in this position where I'm only going to get hurt.

October 17
Watched a movie about this girl who died of cancer (very sad). If someone told me right now that I was going to die soon, I could take it.

October 18
Jane was here this weekend and she is extremely cute and bubbly, so it was very depressing.

October 19
Seems like it wasn't that long ago that I was happy.

October 20
Today is Tommy's sixteenth birthday and we made wishes. Tommy wished to be an artist and be famous. I wished I could travel around the world and everyone would love me. Tommy said, "Can I change my wish to yours?" I wrote a poem for Tommy for his birthday:

> I love Tommy and he loves me,
> So it's plain destiny that we would be
> Never apart. O delight of my heart,
> The real work of art is your fart.

(Tommy is the fart king of the universe. He has gas propulsion.)

October 21
Tommy & I talked about the two of us dating. We decided it would be strange. He said it might work OK if we lived in Paris. I said anything would be OK if we lived in Paris.

October 22
I have this one empty place in my heart that aches. It is plain loneliness.

October 24
Chris asked me out on a date, but Jackson talked it over with me and helped me decide that I'm not going to go.

October 25
I've been thinking a lot about how happy I felt last spring, and about how all of us were so full of the same feelings then, but now

we're not. This is growing up, I guess, accepting that you are on your own.

October 26
I *know* the closeness I have with Jackson is more than friendship, but I don't know if *he* knows it.

October 27
Went mud hogging with Pam in her Bronco and we were bouncing around and tearing down these dirt roads in the woods and we had to winch out of the mud twice. We got filthy and it was a riot! But Pam said she isn't going to prayer meetings anymore because she's sick of Julius telling us how to pray & Jackson's bad temper. She has a point. I mean if we are supposed to acknowledge and overcome our own faults, why should we be blind to theirs?

October 29
Went bowling with a bunch of people and then ate pizza on the levee & discussed creation.

October 30
"I listen to the wind come howl, telling me I have to hurry. I listen to the robin's song saying not to worry."(Cat Stevens) *I'm worried.*

November 1
I'm writing this on November 1 because last night I couldn't write. There were a bunch of Halloween parties, but I didn't go to any of them because I planned to bum with Tommy & Jackson. Then they called and said they couldn't and I don't know why. I keep telling myself not to worry, that God has everything under control. Most everyone didn't go to school today, but I did, so it was an OK day.

November 2

I've gone through terrible doubts about myself over the last six months & I know I'm learning how to manage myself and my emotions, but right now I'm at a loss. I've run the whole thing through my mind a hundred times and I can't fool myself into believing Jackson will *ever* want me.

November 3

The best thing to do is to forge my friendships with girls & make *those* stronger. Right now, I couldn't bear to lose Angela. (I know that sounds queer, but it's true.) I've always felt unattractive to boys and being around Jackson only makes that worse.

(2:41 a.m.) It was a dream. I saw car lights outside the window and knew it was Mother & Daddy back from a trip. Daddy came in and told me he had shot a gun into the woods then later found a canary injured by a gunshot. (But he didn't see any connection between his gunshot & the injured bird.) He was making a clicking noise with something in his hands and I asked what it was and he said bones. "What kind?" I asked. "Human bones," he said.

November 4

My room makes Mama crazy. When I told her that it seems to be in my nature to be messy, she said, "Well then, you better pray to God your nature changes."

November 6

Howdy!! Things are better! Last night I went out with Tommy & Jackson and today I went shopping with Angela. I'm getting along with my parents. I'm feeling great!

November 7

I'm feeling bad.

November 8
Jackson's singing voice is beautiful. It's . . . well, he sounds almost hoarse, as though he's straining, like he's trying to be heard over a wind in his face.

November 9
Tommy is the only person in the world I trust with my emotions. I started crying today just in *fear* that I would lose him.

November 10
We're selling Rex. Jackson is jerking me around. I never know when he's going to show up in my life. Prayer meetings have basically stopped. What's the point of anything?

November 11
Tommy told me Jackson is going to break up with his Shreveport girlfriend. Well, if he starts dating some girl that I have to see him with every day, I might as well join the circus.

November 12
The thing about Jackson is that when I'm with him everything seems better. Tommy and Angela make me happy, but Jackson *thrills* me.

November 13
Got caught skipping French class today but I don't care. I hate French. I honestly think Mrs. Williams should consider changing professions or maybe teaching third graders.

November 14
I'm on a student advisory committee that's supposed to come up with ideas to create good relations between blacks and whites. I'm

the only white girl on the committee and Truck Drummer, who is a senior and the black jock god of Lakewood, is on the committee too. He is so polite. He said hi to me in the hallway today and I had to tell Pam to close her mouth before a fly flew in.

November 15
Today, Mrs. Williams said I have the attention span of a bug.

November 16
All day at school I felt good and it was such a relief. I'm so thankful for my happiness when I feel it.

November 17
Jackson & I rode Rex this morning & watched the sunrise. It was clear and beautiful and we rode until it suddenly clouded up & it rained the whole rest of the day. We went out together tonight and I didn't know how to act with him. I bought a formal dress at a garage sale today for $3.00.

November 18
Trying not to worry about Jackson, but it takes effort, because I know what I want.

November 19
Wanda told me that Doug Reed stuck his hand down her overalls last summer. Can't tell if I'm upset or part of me is jealous.

November 20
I asked Jackson to the Columbus Social Club dance but I'm not sure it was the right thing to do. He made me feel so *low* when I asked, like he was doing me a favor by agreeing to go. On the other hand, I'm feeling stronger lately. I've been talking to other people

about *their* problems and I've found that doing this actually gives me a kind of happiness.

November 21
Today someone came & bought Rex, but they couldn't load him in the trailer because he was rearing and kicking, so they left. I don't think they'll come back.

November 22
I know that God understands what's bothering me—but he's not very good at making conversation about it.

November 23
We lost the playoff game tonight. So this was the last high school football game that Jackson will ever play. I waited with the crowd outside the stadium because I *knew* when Jackson came out & we saw each other something would happen . . . but just as our eyes met, a parent stepped in front of me and grabbed him. WHY? Tonight, I feel like all the football players must feel—that I just have to accept defeat.

November 24
Pam and Angela are not getting along. Pam is being bitchy and says Angela is being a snob. I hope the situation improves.

November 25
Rex tried to kill Jackson. Jackson walked into the pen and Rex let him get right up close with the halter and then *swoosh*, Rex wheeled around and kicked Jackson in the chest and knocked him flat! I almost fainted! Luckily, the hoof hit right in the middle of his sternum, and all he has is a bad bruise. (If he had been short, it would have hit him in the *head*.) Afterward, we ate lunch at

Jackson's house. There's something about the Bishops' house that makes me feel uncomfortable. Maybe because it's always so clean.

November 26
At the basketball game, Jackson purposely flirted with other girls right in front of me. Now I'm thinking it's too bad Rex didn't bruise his face a little.

November 27
I'm glad my sisters are home. I know this is stupid . . . but when the three of us went shopping today, they hardly paid any attention to me. Of course they have more to talk about, being in college and closer in age.

November 28
I went for a walk in the park today and felt so mad at myself for not being able to tell people how I feel.

November 29
We sold Rex. Son-of-a-bitch cowboy from Slidell bought him.

December 1
Drove to Moon Lake with Tommy & Jackson & we built a fire & were having a fun time until Jackson said that only people who accept Jesus Christ go to heaven. I argued (What about Jews?) and Jackson said, "I didn't make the rules, Maggie. Jesus did."

December 2
I've figured out that my biggest hang-up is that I'm scared to death of loneliness. I *know* I need to overcome this, but the fear of being in a position of *having* to overcome it is what really worries me.

December 3

I need to get over not dating and not let it bother me. But I would still *like* to date, or at least have a date *occasionally*.

December 4

Today in P.E. all the girls were gossiping like hyenas. How is it possible *not* to hate school?

December 5

Mama suggested I read *Walden* and left her copy on my bed with a note. She wrote that "sometimes the confusion and complexity of our lives gets in the way and we forget what is really basic and important and this book helps put things in perspective."

December 6

Attended a funeral. I don't enjoy funerals but I think I understand them.

December 7

I was with Pam all day and got home around 7 p.m. Jackson called and he was mad because he had been trying to find me all day to go to the movies. We went for a walk on the levee and I wanted to tell him things, but then I didn't.

December 8

Jackson's dog Hector was hit by a car and killed. He *loved* that dog. It tore him apart. As soon as I heard, I went over to his house & Tommy was already there & Jackson was *out of his mind* crying. We helped bury Hector but we couldn't reach Jackson. He had to be alone with it.

December 9
I am so fed up with myself! I never do anything right! I checked out of school & came home & cleaned up my room and dresser. I don't see how I can face another day of school.

December 10
Jackson seemed better when I saw him at church but he was different. I sensed it. Like he has grown up and away from me.

December 11
"I went to the woods because I wished to live deliberately . . . ." (Henry David Thoreau)

December 12
Because of all my unexcused absences, I had to walk around the school grounds all afternoon picking up trash with a poker and a bag. It was a *little* bit embarrassing.

December 13
Jackson doesn't want me. I'm not going to feel sorry for myself about this. I'm going to accept it.

December 14
I don't know where to begin or how it happened or if it should have happened. Today, Jackson & I went to the park & it seemed we weren't afraid anymore. After walking around and playing for a while, we lay on the ground and I had my head on his stomach & we watched the clouds. Oddly, I wasn't thinking about Jackson. I'd already accepted that nothing was going to happen between us. That was when he asked me to go out with him tonight. We decided to go to the youth hut where we could be alone & we ended up snuggled up lying down together. Then we went back to Jackson's house

but instead of going inside, we sat in his car. We talked about our hang-ups & I told him about my fear of loneliness & he said his biggest hang-up was that he was *conceited*. He said he was a good person for the wrong reasons, that he's good because he wants to impress people & hear them say, "Oh, look what a good Christian Jackson is." He said he *always* worries about what people think of him. I'm glad I know Jackson better, but after we got so close & all at the hut, I felt dirty, like I had done something wrong.

December 15
Jesus, please let me grow up right now! I need to grow away from the world, so I will not be pulled in by its glamour and deceit and *false* promises.

December 17
Satan came closer to me tonight than I've ever felt & it scared me and Tommy out of our heads. We were sitting in Tommy's car in his driveway & it *hit* me & I was almost *hallucinating*.

December 18
Jackson & I are going to a party this weekend. It's very important that I find a dress to wear that I feel comfortable in.

December 19
Tommy told me that Betsy has been overly jealous at school and even mean to him.

December 20
Went to a Christmas party with Jackson. We felt stupid (really, only I felt stupid) and decided to go for a walk on the levee instead. We kissed, and it should have been romantic, and I tried to believe it was, but it was only cold and uncomfortable.

December 21

Well, it's 2:30 a.m. I just got home from the Knights of Columbus Christmas Formal. Jackson and I went parking tonight and it was so *intimate*. At the dance, though, it seemed like Jackson was trying not to pay too much attention to me. He didn't put his arm around me or anything. I was hurt. He wasn't watching me dance; he was looking around. He was thinking about something and I don't know what it was.

December 23

Tonight Jackson took me to the Interact Club keg party and all his old friends and their girlfriends were there. It was OK, but I was uncomfortable. Maybe this is dumb, but all the girls there were so cute & fun & I'm so gross & dull. I can't talk to those people & I don't see how Jackson could even begin to like me. I'm going to cling to him though.

December 24

Jackson dropped by and handed me a Christmas present all wrapped. I was so excited that I opened it in my room right after he left. It was some dried flowers under glass. I mean, it's nice, but it's a *dead plant*.

December 25

I got a nice new winter coat—not as nice as my old coat, but nice.

December 28

Mama and Daddy are always telling me what to do. I don't want conflict, but I can't seem to do what they want.

December 29

I am *not* infatuated with Jackson. I'm in *love* with him.

December 30

       Where are you, Love? What must I do?
       You snap. I leap. You say. I do. You change.
       I stay the same—It's true.

December 31

I'm terrified of what's happening to me. I spent a fantastic afternoon in the park with Jackson today, just the two of us, and it was
wonderful. Then at church tonight he was almost ignoring me.
Well, that's not true, it's just that he just wasn't giving me any special attention . . . that's because he was giving it all to a girl named
Patty. God, I'm *hurting!* This is all wrong. In between the times
we're so close, Jackson acts as though I'm nobody special. It's past
midnight and 1974 is gone. This year has taught me an *awful lot.*

1975

"Blind Man's Bluff"

January 1

"Happy New Year, Maggie! I love you and wanted you to wake up this morning and read this." Tommy left that note taped to the back door. He came over and we talked about how neat it is that a boy and girl can be as close as we are and not be anything more than friends. I'm going with Jackson to some parties today and I feel queasy about it.

(later) Felt totally out of place at the football party. This bogged-down feeling I've had the last few days is getting to me. Something's gotta happen.

January 2

Something happened. Tommy told me that he talked to Jackson and Jackson says he thinks we should stop spending so much time together and that we should go back to being just friends. —I'm in hell. I am in hell but I am not dead. *I wish I were dead.* It would hurt less.

January 3

"My heart is smitten, and withered like grass . . ." (Psalm 102)

Fasted yesterday—and this morning I almost threw up when Mama made me eggs and bacon. I've been thinking that in church they tell us we are the last generation and the world could end any day, and if that's true, then there is a reason life is so difficult.

January 4

Tonight, watching the sunset, it was like seeing a city of gold, castles, and roads in the clouds, like heaven. I was watching heaven for half an hour. By the end of it, I felt I had been chosen somehow . . . that heaven had been revealed *just for me.*

January 5

I'm not dreading school tomorrow. I'm at peace. It's that kind of *full* feeling of peace that makes you want to hold still . . . afraid that if you move, the peace will smother you.

January 6

I've decided to improve myself and give 100% of myself to everything I do—and towards other people, too. I did end up skipping P.E. & lunch today. Was that wrong? Is skipping unimportant classes wrong?

January 7

At school, someone passed around a message, and when the bell rang for second period, every white kid in the school went and sat in the auditorium. It was pretty hilarious. I'm glad when anything makes school more bearable.

January 8

I walked outside in the dark and heard a dog cry. It sounded just like a child, a crazed child.

January 9

RANDOM OBSERVATIONS

My mother is beautiful.

My father is smart.

My brother is a perfect example of the careless charm of boys.

I can't carry a tune.

The dots on my bedroom ceiling only connect in my head.

The stars in the sky are not dots.

Life is dark.

Love can be blind.

Being in the dark is not the same as being blind.

January 10

I saw so many people die in a movie tonight (*The Towering Inferno*) that I started crying & praying for them. Mary called to say she is getting married and she wants me and Stella to be bridesmaids.

January 11

I believe that Jackson let something *real* drop out of his life for the *wrong* reasons—and I think he *knows* it.

January 12

Watched the Super Bowl with Tommy and Jackson. The strong attraction to Jackson is still there, but feeling so much love can't be a *bad* thing?

January 13

I went to school & the day flew by. Had a hard Geometry test & flew through it. I've decided to accept myself & not feel ugly or inferior.

January 14

I made a 100 in Geometry. Loving Jackson *doesn't* mean that I want him. I want only God. We played in the snow—it snowed today!

January 15

Found Mama asleep on the living room sofa again this morning. I'm afraid of losing my friends, and my fears control me too much. I wish I could separate myself from the world.

January 16

Heard that the singer Al Green's girlfriend poured boiling grits on him and then killed herself, which seems strange. Found out that Jackson asked Rhonda to the football banquet and she asked him to the Y-teens dance, which seems wrong.

January 17
Tommy took me to hear this famous speaker at the Assembly of
God revival tonight, but I wasn't moved—not to joy, sadness, anything. I'm lost and a little afraid. I can't believe that Jackson is
dating *Rhonda* . . . I mean she's nice and sort of pretty, but she's
dumb as grits.

January 18
Went back to the revival with Tommy and people were falling down
and feeling the spirit and speaking in tongues and I TRIED. I was
searching, searching for I don't know what. I went to the altar
once, then twice, and still nothing. Jackson was there with Rhonda,
fussing over her, and I could *see* them from where I was sitting and
suddenly it *dawned* on me . . . that Jackson never expected to get
as close to me as he did and he never *wanted* to. When I understood
that, I started crying & laughing at the same time. That was when
Tommy took me out of the church, and on the way home, God
spoke to me. He told me that I have to grow up. It's *time*.

January 19
Met Tommy in the driveway at 7 a.m. and we walked to the park. It
was cold but exhilarating! Then we ran into Julius. I don't know
what it is with Julius but he scares me. Sometimes he comes on too
strong and I don't know how to cope and I'm really mean to him.
He *bugs* me. But I'm sure he'll be a good minister and Oral Roberts
University will be perfect for him, because Oral Roberts bugs
me, too.

January 20
Tonight, lying in bed, I had a vision that I was in heaven with
Jesus. I said to Jesus, "Isn't anyone else here?" Jesus said, "Isn't
this enough?" So I looked around and saw there were shelves,

endless shelves with people lying on them, mostly kids, and they were all dead.

January 21

Conversation with Mama after church:

ME: If you don't believe in God, why do you go to church?

MAMA: Because I've always *wanted* to believe in God, Margaret. I just have never been able to.

ME: So what do you believe?

MAMA: I don't know. I can't answer that.

ME: Are you an atheist?

MAMA: Oh . . . no. I wouldn't want to call myself that.

ME: Well, what does Daddy believe?

MAMA: I think Daddy believes in God, but I don't think he would ever talk about it.

ME: Why not?

MAMA: Because, Margaret, it's just one of those things.

January 22

Today in P.E. Pam and Hallie were sitting on the bleachers near me & talking about all their troubles, and Pam looked at me and said, "Well, Margaret, must be nice not to have any worries." I said, "It sure is." And then they went back to their conversation. This is what I learned today: Some girls are like *fucking* bats in daylight.

January 23

Mama took me with her to the Old Folks' Home to visit Miss Inez because she didn't want to go there alone. Miss Inez is an old friend of Momma Doll's and Mama has known her since she was a little girl. Miss Inez's family couldn't take care of her anymore because she gets confused and so now she is living there. It was awful. The whole place smells like disinfectant. There was an old lady in the other bed that looked unconscious. Miss Inez asked us several times if we'd have breakfast with her even though it was the afternoon. When we finally said we had to go, she said, "Well, I expect I'll go with you." Mama said, "No, you have to stay here a while, Miss Inez. They need to do some tests." (The part about the tests wasn't true.)

MISS INEZ: "They thought that at first, you know, but then they decided I should go home."

MAMA: "No, you're supposed to stay here. They have a room for you."

MISS INEZ: (looking around) "It's not a very big room."

MAMA: "But it's *your* room, and your daughter is coming to see you very soon."

MISS INEZ: "Well then, I expect she'll take me home. Because I *need* to get home." Then she leaned over and whispered, "They can't keep us *all* here."

It was the saddest place I've ever been.

January 24
Jackson's girlfriend Rhonda was voted junior class favorite & so was her ex-boyfriend Bobby D.

January 25
GREAT weekend!

January 26
GREAT WEATHER!

January 27
I'd like to get to know Bobby D. better.

January 29
I'm *completely* over Jackson. I'm not even going to think about us maybe getting back together again. The fact that I never have dates doesn't bother me either. I actually don't think I should date in high school. I don't think it would be good for me.

January 30
Mama left today on a skiing trip to Colorado and Daddy decided not to go. I saw Jackson and Rhonda today and it didn't hurt in the slightest bit. But then when I thought about it, I almost started crying.

January 31
What I've realized lately is that *love* is not as I thought it was. It doesn't free you; it binds you. It has a million strings that wrap around you, but love itself can't *be* bound—because it's a yearning and a desire you can't control. So you can't so much search for love, as release yourself to it, and then accept the consequences.

February 1
Bad day. Loneliness. What I don't understand is why are Jackson and Rhonda *happy*, while I'm so *unhappy?*

February 2
WHAT MAKES ME HAPPY
being with Angela
being with Tommy
being in the woods

WHAT MAKES ME UNHAPPY
Being bored
Being ignored
French class

February 3

I got my braces off! Went over to show Tommy and he said I looked *beautiful!* Then Ellen said she wanted to give me a makeup lesson. Ellen thinks my eyebrows look like caterpillars crawling across my face. She says you don't dress up and wear makeup for yourself, you do it for the people who have to look at you. (Talked to Mama on the phone.)

February 4

Ellen Townsend's bathroom is like in a *fairy tale*—or like what a bathroom would look like if fairy tales *had* bathrooms. It's a long rectangle shape with a red carpet on the floor and a long white marble counter running along one wall with a huge mirror that goes from the counter to the ceiling. The other side of the room has a white tile built-in tub and shower. I sat on a stool covered in red velvet while she plucked my eyebrows and showed me how to put on eye shadow and where the apple of my cheek was. She taught me to separate my eyelashes with a straight pin and told me I should wear my hair in a ponytail, not a braid. When I walked out, Tommy said it was like seeing Clark Kent come out of a phone booth. He pretended to faint. When I walked in the back door of my house and Bill saw me, he said, "You clean up real good."

February 5

I was joking around with Tony in study hall and he asked me out for two dates—this weekend and the Heart Fund dance. I was surprised, but I'm not complaining.

February 6

Tommy's dinner party was the most fun I've *ever* had. I wore a long rust-colored jersey halter dress. Ellen helped me put on makeup and she fixed my hair in a bun on top of my head. Jackson & Rhonda being there didn't hurt in the least bit at all because Jackson and I have become so separate. Completely. I barely talked to him. Angela & I flew a kite this afternoon and got it 2,600 feet high.

February 7
Ellen threw out my favorite coat from the Salvation Army because she hated it. (I kind of loved it.) I had FUN with Tony tonight, but we went parking and he started saying how he thought about me all the time and I couldn't help laughing. It was such a *line.* I miss Mama. I wish she were here.

February 8
Tony hugs me a lot. He treats me the way I would want a boy to treat me—he's just the wrong boy.

February 9
My mother is safely home from her ski trip. Daddy built a fire in the fireplace & the house was nice & warm when she got here.

February 10
Seeing Jackson's car in Tommy's driveway is like seeing a padlock on Tommy's back door.

February 11
This afternoon when I couldn't find the keys to my locked car, and when I had to go back into the Piggly Wiggly to look for them, I *knew* it was for a reason. Then I ran into Jackson and Rhonda who were just walking in, and it *hit* me. Jackson isn't the same Jackson I loved and I'm not the same Margaret either.

February 12
Wanda agrees with me that Jackson has become less Jackson-like.
Now he's so *normal*. I remember when I first fell in love with Jackson. It was during a prayer meeting on the levee at sunset. Now at
sunset, I don't think of love anymore—I think of loneliness.

February 13
Tony calls every night. Betsy wrote me a note that said she thinks
the devil is keeping her and Tommy apart.

February 14
Betsy sent me a Valentine & signed it, "I'll see ya at the Rapture!"

February 15
Tony and I went parking for one & a half hours but I don't feel
dirty or anything. It's fun. That's all it is.

February 16
I'm beginning to like this part of growing up.

February 17
Things are turning around for me.

February 18
At Black History assembly today, everyone was supposed to stand
up and sing "We Shall Overcome" but a bunch of white kids refused to sing or stand up. (I think Eddie Owens started it.) It was
embarrassing. It made me want to apologize to people like Coach
Baylor. When I told Mama that, she was surprised. Then I realized
that all this time Mama has been picturing Coach Baylor as *white*.
I can't get over that.

February 19

Why is it harder for me to relax around the people I love? That's scary to me.

February 20

I got caught skipping class. Tony let the air out of a teacher's tires because she gave him a bad grade. I exchanged my new top at Selber's around 5 p.m. & accidentally got locked inside the store. When I *finally* found someone to let me out, I discovered I had locked my keys in the car! For some reason, it all felt hilarious!

February 21

Well, it's 1:30 a.m. and I just got home from the Heart Fund dance. I have some problems. At the dance I went wild & everyone thought I was drunk. (Some people even asked me if I was drunk.) All I wanted was to have a good time. I saw a bunch of drunk people tonight & why do they do it? I can see perfectly clearly why. Because they feel fake & drinking is not a crutch, not like I *thought*. I see *now* that drinking releases that protective covering each of us has & lets the person out . . . cracks the shell around them. I've got a shell & I hide under it *hating* myself. I want to throw the shell away & get rid of it. I want to accept who I am.

February 22

Woke up at noon, washed my hair, and am sitting under a hot hair dryer with my hair in rollers. I'm mixed up about certain things— like those speakers at church revivals & the healings & are they for *real*? Is it *God* that moves them?

PLACES I HATE TO BE:
My room when it's messy
Under hair dryers

PEOPLE I WISH I COULD KNOW:
Jesus
Emily Dickinson
Walter Cronkite

FAVORITE BOOKS:
The Bible (King James)
The Poems of Emily Dickinson
In Cold Blood (Truman Capote)

BOOKS I DON'T LIKE:
My French textbook
The Exorcist

February 23
People are treating me differently lately. Boys are. The song "Best
of My Love" reminds me of Angela.

February 24
Didn't talk to Tony all day. Maybe he doesn't want to go out with
me anymore. I don't care.

February 25
Skipped school & saw Tony, who was also skipping school. I was
on my bike and he was in his Cutlass. He took me to breakfast at
Sambo's, so I guess he still likes me.

February 26
Boys have been paying a lot of attention to me at school, which I
like, but it causes some problems.

February 27
Part of me feels like I failed with Jackson.

February 28
Went to a concert at the Civic Center and all the girls drank & some of them got drunk. I'm with them and they're my friends. I act crazy & drink. I have a good time. Is it so wrong?

March 1
I've been cussing more lately and out loud. I'm worried that Bill isn't getting along with Daddy and that Daddy doesn't listen to him. I need to watch myself. I wish I could reach down in my heart and pull out the BAD stuff that should not be there and throw it away.

March 2
Betsy told me she saw a photograph taken by a woman who was on a trip with her husband. The woman pointed the camera out the window and took a picture of the clouds. Later that day, they had a car accident and the wife was killed and when the husband developed the pictures, you could see Jesus in the clouds with his arms outstretched. I would like to see that picture.

March 3
I spent all day Sunday with Beau, a boy I've been going out with some. He's sweet and I like him, but he's an alcoholic.

March 4
I was paying my tab at the Grill and the new waitress Esther stared at the cash register and said out loud to no one, "I have no idea what I'm doing." Then Fanny, the old waitress, looked over and said, "None of us do, honey. None of us do."

March 5
Went out with Beau last night and woke up with a *terrible* headache (and skinned knees?).

March 6
These are touchy times.

March 7
I think I'm going to have to dynamite Jackson's car. It's the only way I can figure out to keep from having to see it parked in Tommy's driveway all the time.

March 11
Been sick & sleeping in Mama & Daddy's bed while they took Stella back to New Orleans. Stella wants to find a job but doesn't know how to go about it. She thinks it's Mama's fault. Right now I feel like I'm ugly, just an ugly person.

March 12
Stella is a hard person to figure out. Once last fall, I asked her to feed Rex for me and she thought I was kidding. She said, "You've got to be kidding." Stuff like that makes it difficult to get along with her.

March 13
Beau kisses me in front of other people and I don't like it. Too many boys are calling & I feel passed around. This is no good.

March 14
This afternoon I went over to say hi to Jackson in Tommy's driveway and he very clearly gave me the "bug off" message. I really hate how fat my cheeks are. I look like a chipmunk.

March 15
The old bridge is closed. A barge ran into it and knocked part of it off into the river. The new bridge makes me nervous because it's

very wide, and when it ices over, boys like to drive cars fast to the middle, brake, and then spin the steering wheel to see how many times they can spin the car around. It seems to me that most boys are born stupid.

March 16
Went to the Holiday Inn Grill with Angela. I was in a good mood. I played the "William Tell Overture" (the *Lone Ranger* theme song) *twice* on the jukebox and Angela said I was embarrassing her. Angela's shyness can be deafening.

March 17
Mother committed suicide in my dream. She was upstairs with a man (not Daddy) & she jumped out the window. I knew that Mama didn't really love this other man, but she liked him & she just sort of fell into being with him. Then some men in white robes (like the KKK) walked up and I was scared to death & said in my most friendly voice, "I'm from Louisiana." They didn't seem impressed so I got frantic and said, "My mother has either committed suicide or been murdered!" "Why?" the KKK men asked, but I thought they meant *why* was she having an affair & I tried to explain that she was a woman and she had *needs* and I pointed to them and said, "like *you*," and they burst out laughing.

March 18
Wanda has been smoking pot & hanging out with people using speed & hard stuff. She says she's quitting.

March 19
I haven't written about this because I don't want to believe it, but my mother & father are not communicating. They're just not the same as they were. Mama's been crying lately and Daddy's gone a

lot. They avoid each other & when they do talk, it's all fake. It's tearing me apart.

March 20

Went out to Alto with Daddy to take some pictures and a man at Gilley's Store said we should head over near Vicksburg where people get together and dress up like Rebel soldiers. He said for one weekend a year, they eat like 'em and cook like 'em. They wear those costumes and "re-activate the war."

March 23

Last night I babysat a five-year-old and she asked what a "wreck" was. I told her it was when things smash into each other. She was quiet for a second and then said, "Then I know what a rectangle is." I said, "What is it?" She said, "It's when two squares *wreck*, and then they *tangle*."

March 24

Trying to take one day at a time.

March 25

I've decided to try out for the Bengal Belles, the high-kick dance squad at Monroe High. They're kind of like the June Taylor dancers on the *Jackie Gleason Show*, except that they do all their dances standing up. There are twenty-one girls chosen by judges. Betsy is already a Bengal Belle. I think I'd like it.

March 26

Big blow-up in the driveway! Beau rode a motorcycle over to the house and Daddy made him leave. Then Daddy told me if he ever caught me on a motorcycle with a boy, I'd be grounded until I got married. (It appears that Daddy does not like Beau.)

March 28
Today old Mr. Parker was walking by himself on the side of Loop
Road and Mama stopped to give him a ride home. (He's sort of se-
nile and gets lost.) He said we could give him a ride, but not all the
way home. We took him home anyway, but when I walked him to
the door of his house, his wife answered and said, "Oh no, don't
bring him home. He's fine."

March 30
I went boat riding with Tony in Hog Bayou after church & then
we got stuck in the spillway & the motor wouldn't start and we had
to walk back. It was cold but nice. Mama is sick. I think she has
the flu.

March 31
There was a sniper shooting in West Monroe & some people were
killed.

April 1
Lately I've become so self-conscious around other girls. Everyone
loves Angela and I feel like a tagalong.

April 3
My stomach is hurting again and Beau thinks I have an ulcer. (He
had one.)

April 4
River View Academy is so rinky-dink that in order to have enough
people show up for their prom, they sent out invitations to seniors
at other schools. Jackson got invited and he asked me to go with
him. Strange.

April 5

Beau and I were sitting on the levee today and he was tickling me & suddenly I realized my bra was undone. I think he did it on purpose.

April 6

I had the *worst* time at the prom with Jackson. If only he had treated me like a date! I was insulted! I got mad a few times & walked off, but he deserved it. Big boy! *He* asked *me*. I wasn't chasing him and I sure don't want to go back to him. The whole night just felt wrong. (The fact that I didn't have time to buy a dress and Mama convinced me to wear an old polka-dot bridesmaid dress that Mary wore last summer only made it *worse*.) Jackson didn't even kiss me good night! Right now dating him is *completely* out of the question.

April 7

I woke up at 5 a.m. this morning & couldn't get back to sleep, so I left a note saying I went to Angela's early to study & took off on my bike with a notebook & some money. I ended up at Betsy's house around 6:30 a.m. and knocked on her window to wake her up & she let me in the house. I stayed there & ate breakfast. (Her mother didn't act too surprised when I walked in the kitchen from Betsy's bedroom.) Betsy drove me to the youth hut and dropped me off on the way to school. I called school from the church kitchen & tried to pretend I was my mother, but Mrs. Walker, the secretary, recognized my voice & told me to either go home or come to school or she had to call my parents. So I called Mama & told her where I was & that I was clearing my head & wasn't going to school. She tried to understand. (I begged her not to tell Daddy but she said she had to.) I slept some & read some & thought & prayed & wrote. Pastor Bob came in & saw me, but didn't say much. Mama came to see me for a few minutes but I couldn't explain it to her and she left. Betsy came after school & brought me something to eat & I let her take me to Momma Doll's, then Momma Doll brought me home. I know I think too much about myself. I compare myself with other people. I've *got* to change, to begin by treating people the way I want them to treat me . . . to not expect from someone else what I myself wouldn't do. I've decided I'm going to help retarded kids this summer.

April 8
Got suspended from school for too many unexcused absences, twelve counting yesterday. They sent me home and I can't come back until Thursday. Mama & Daddy don't seem very mad. It didn't faze me a bit.

April 9
Stayed home. Mama and Daddy haven't tried to talk to me and I'm so glad.

April 10
I'm still grounded.

April 11
Threw the polka-dot dress in the garbage. Cut it into little bitty pieces first.

April 12
Feel unstable. Wish I could just settle down. Jackson is 18 years old today.

April 13
I feel an odd yearning. I want to rekindle my friendship with Jackson.

April 14
Back in school.

April 15
Jackson called. We have a date this weekend. (?)

April 16
Mama & Daddy went out to dinner and when they got back, Bill was asleep but I was watching the *Tonight Show*. The two of them sat down on either side of me on the couch and then Daddy said, "We want to talk to you." My heart was pounding away at my ribcage and Daddy started talking and Mama started quietly crying. Daddy said I was going to have a little brother or sister. I said, "What do you mean?" He said, "Your mother is pregnant." I about fainted. I looked at Mama and asked did she *want* to have a baby, and she said, "Well, no, Margaret, but there's nothing we can do." So I said, "Haven't you ever heard of having your tubes tied?" Daddy said (kind of irritated), "Your mother is going to be *fine*, but she'll need *your* help." I tried to say something else, but Daddy cut me off and they went to bed. He said we can't tell anyone about Mama for another month. I ate two bowls of ice cream and six Oreos. *Why* is this happening? I don't want this to mess up all our lives.

April 17
I can't believe my mother is pregnant. She's *forty-four* and Daddy is *fifty-four* and a lot could go wrong. They're *too* old. We all are.

April 18
I went out to eat with Jackson tonight. But a date to Jackson is friendly to me. He doesn't touch or show any affection.

April 19

Tommy & Jackson wanted me to go on a picnic, but I went out with Beau instead. Being around Jackson, I think it's bad for me. But Beau isn't the right person for me either, because he's a juvenile delinquent. I care about Beau and his friends, but I'm not sure what I'm doing hanging out with these people.

April 20

Mama is *very* sick. She says she was this sick with every pregnancy but I find that hard to believe. I'm so discouraged about Bengal Belles. It became clear to me today that I want to be a Bengal Belle dancer more than anything I've ever wanted. And caring this much is potentially very bad for me.

April 21

It finally dawned on me that Beau has been *using* me to make his old girlfriend jealous. I'd like to kick him so he can't have children, but I don't want to give him the satisfaction of thinking his existence in the universe matters to me. I need to come down to reality. What I'd *like* to do is to crawl into a different reality, someplace warm and secure, but that doesn't exist so I can't.

April 22

I wish I could make Mama better but I can't even talk to her.

April 23

I've been putting all my energy into practicing for BB dance try-outs and I'm trying to prepare myself to be disappointed. If I don't make it, I want to be able to accept it. And if I do make it, I'll be SO happy, but not everyone can.

April 24

Stella & Mary are coming in town tomorrow. They have no idea how tense it's been around here. What if something is wrong with Mama's baby? She's so sick. It scares me all the time.

April 25

I can't believe it! I'm so grateful! (I feel bad for the people who didn't make it.) I'm a Bengal Belle! A DANCER! After tryouts I almost cut my finger off, and I've got four stitches in it. Angela and Pam made the BB squad too. I'm so excited! It was a beautiful day! We were all going for Cokes after tryouts and were putting down the top on Angela's VW bug & when I reached in to push back the canvas, Angela slammed the top down and my finger got caught in the hinge. I still had on the white gloves from tryouts and when I took out my hand, there was bright red blood soaking through. Angela took me to the ER & I was more afraid than I was hurt because I knew it was a bad cut and broken also. When we got there, I told them my name and there was no wait, no forms or anything, and Uncle Henry walked in & sewed my finger back on and put it in a splint (which is why this handwriting is so bad). When I got home I was so *happy*, but everyone at the house was in a *bad, serious mood* so I didn't say much. Mary wrecked her car driving in from Dallas and Mother was lying on the couch sick and my father has so much on his mind. Mary and Stella cornered me in the kitchen & told me it would be selfish to do BBs because it would be too time consuming & I should be helping Mama. *No one in my family has any idea how important this is to me.* I think (hope) Mama understands. I can't believe I almost cut off my finger! The painkiller is wearing off. It's really starting to hurt.

April 28

My finger is better. It's still hard to write with a splint on. I'm kind of depressed. Daddy is tense & my mother cries.

April 30
I can poke a pin in my fingertip and not feel it.

May 1
A bone usually heals, but when a nerve is severed, it doesn't always grow back. Just like a broken heart.

May 5
My stitches are out. I'm practicing with the Bengal Belles every day after school now. I need to slow down and spend some time at home. I have to face what's going on there.

May 7
Mama gets so mad at everyone! I can't do anything right! I know it's not entirely her fault & she's sick & depressed, but she won't let me do a thing!

May 8
Tonight Mama and I had another big fight and I was so upset that she came into my room later & apologized.

May 9
Daddy thinks I should be at home, but I don't want to be at home. And there's nothing I can do to make Mama feel better anyway.

May 10
Mama told me she has nightmares where babies are clinging to her like little monkeys or are being taken from her, or are being hurt and killed or kidnapped.

May 11

I told Jackson my mother was pregnant while we were in the TG&Y parking lot. He jumped out of the car, flung his arms around, and started talking about the *possibilities & consequences* of it. Then he got back in the car and talked the rest of the time about his dilemma at taking the step out of high school & into college. I think I might be falling apart.

May 12

No one else understands what's going on here, except Bill. A sophomore named Dash Miller called and asked me out for this weekend, which was kind of a surprise because he's a big football star. Oh well.

May 13

Every day when I come home from school, Mama is lying on the sofa looking pale and sad and she always wants me to sit and talk to her, but I don't want to. Then she gets mad at me and says I don't care.

May 15

I prayed so hard for my family last night that I fell asleep praying. Stella and Mary make things worse by telling me what I should do. I try hard, but I could try a bit harder.

May 16

Mary's wedding announcement tea was today. It was at the Browns' house and it was so boring that I wandered around the house looking for books to read.

May 17

I had a GREAT time with Dash and he asked me out again for Saturday night! Should I have played more hard-to-get? I got a

little drunk. I'm not sure how to conduct myself on a date anymore.

May 18
Jesus, are you watching over me? (I hope someone is.)

May 19
Poor Mr. Parker was wandering down the street and got hit by a car
and killed.

May 20
I'm comfortable with Dash. He *likes* me. This is the first time I've
ever felt secure with any boy.

May 21
We were thinking up names for the baby and Daddy said my name
means "pearl." Bill went and looked it up, and he said the *World
Book Encyclopedia Dictionary* says my name means "scales with a
pearly luster." So I looked up Bill's name and the first definition
was "horny mouth of a bird." Then Daddy made us stop.

May 22
Jackson and I are going out Friday night, whatever that means. I'm
not getting along with my family. I feel guilty because it's so depressing at my house that I just want to get away from it. Also, my
relationship with Dash is moving very fast. I need to use some
common sense.

May 24
Dash & I were watching TV at my house & I had my head in his lap
on the couch and was sort of running my hand up and down his

calf when I felt something start *moving* under my ear. I didn't know what it was, so I kept running my hand up and down, up and down, and then Dash got up—and then he left—and then I knew.

May 26
Report cards not so good. Daddy will be mad.

May 27
Daddy signed my report cards without saying anything. He has a lot on his mind.

May 28
I was with some friends floating on rafts on the bayou today, and it seemed very relaxing, but I started crying. I had to leave and couldn't explain it to anyone. I suppose something touched it off but I don't know what it was. Jackson invited me to go out to his family farm with him on Friday.

May 29
Dash said he loved me. He called me long-distance from Florida. I need to set him straight when he gets back. We're having fun together, that's all it is.

May 30
All right, Jesus, only *you* will understand what I'm talking about. It's *happened*. I've known for so many months, but I buried it. Now the stone has been rolled away! I'm talking about me & Jackson. We both know there is something real between us, ahead of us, *waiting* for us. Today at his farm, we were thinking the same thoughts. And now I have a decision to make, because Dash wants to get more serious.

May 31

Jackson came over today and we didn't mention yesterday. I went out with Tony. I was in an upset mood though. There's something Jackson said that keeps running through my mind. He said, "It's not that I'm just super crazy about you, but that you make me *happy.*"

June 1

Dash is home from Florida and he came over. I like Dash. Jackson leaves in less than a week and we haven't talked about what's happening between us.

June 2

I wrote Jackson a letter in a notebook that I'm going to leave in his car in the morning on the way to BB dance practice.

Monday night, June 2

Hey Baby, It's 12:31 a.m. I need to sleep but I can't. Here it is: By being with you, I'm hurting the possibilities of other relationships, and part of me worries that you're only being with me to prove something. Are you?

Jackson, when I'm calm, I believe what I feel for you is sincere and I would like to overcome the problems between us. But I also believed I could make a rational decision about "us" after you left. Now, I realize there's not going to be a decision for me, because I'm not going to be able to let go of you—and that is so fucking scary for me.

The point is (and you know this) that I am always trying to look *past the surface* of things, and that's what I'm trying to do with this situation. I do believe that love can hold up against the waves of time, even mistrust and anger, and maybe we have that kind of love, but I don't know yet.

I need to know what you're thinking. Write back and give me back the notebook.

I love you, Margaret

6-3-75

Maggie, I didn't know if you wanted me to write in here, but here goes: I wrote a poem last night in my notebook, this morning I ripped it out. It was a good poem; kind of silly, but serious. I didn't like it because it was just too much me and too much you, just us, like there was nothing else, or rather, no one else to it. Well, it's a crazy situation but I think it's pretty good. The end. Loving you, Jackson.

P.S. I'm really happy now. You're a pretty kid. Hang in there. Let's—well, I've said most all—maybe someday—forget it. I don't really want to say good-bye. Bye. I heard what you said in what you wrote, I think. We don't know anything. And I've got a lot to say, but I don't think I can say it unless I say it with my life. I think it's gonna be alright. Don't you? Can you hear what I'm saying? Love ya, Jackson Bishop.

Tuesday night—
Dear Jackson,
Is this as hard for you as it is for me? Do you think you know me?

Everyone thinks I'm so strong, but I'm not. I've learned to protect myself, and I suppose that's a kind of strength, but not the best kind. Let me put it this way: I prepare for the worst and most people terrify me. I'm even afraid of you. I find it very difficult to trust people with my real feelings. There are *some* times when I'm not terribly self-conscious, and my emotions aren't bottled up, and those are the times when I'm close to happiness. At times, I've felt very happy with you.

The hardest part to explain is that I'm afraid to love you because I might cling to you and you might not really want me. What's worse, though, is that while I find it hard to trust *you*, I fully expect you to trust *me*. It's unfair, but that's the way I feel. This leads me to the part about Dash. I promise that I won't let him interfere with these next few days I have with you, but I'm asking you to understand that Dash is another world to me and I can't make any promises. What I can *honestly* say is that you are in my heart, and I couldn't get you out, even when I most wanted to.

This is probably the strangest love letter ever written.

You have my love,

Margaret

P.S. "Let us lay aside every weight, and the sin which doth so easily beset us, and let us run with patience the race that is set before us." (Hebrews 12:1)

6-4-75

Maggie, I know what you're thinking and it's good; I feel the same way about a lot of things. I understand about this summer, and even next year. I know it's tough. And to me, besides being just a tiny bit silly, I think you're one of the best kids around. I had a bunch of fun at the party tonight; you looked really pretty—you always do, but I mean you looked like good ol' Maggie, ya know? Don't think much

about me this summer; it won't be that long. I'm gonna
really miss Tommy, too. It's good. I'm pretty bottled up,
too, Marg. That's what I meant by the first couple of
sentences. I ask myself, "Is it wrong?" I don't think so—I
have a lot down in me; some of it is very personal, private.
You know 'cause you do too and that's what makes you,
you, and me, me. 'Night, J.B. Love.

June 4

Well, I've spent the whole week with Jackson, every moment we
could manage, but I'm still afraid to believe that he might truly
care for me. Dash has called twice in the last three days but I
haven't called back. Then there's Tommy, who doesn't understand
what's going on, because we haven't talked, and we should have.

Thursday night
Dear Tommy,
I thank God every night for you and your friendship. I
know I take you for granted sometimes and I'm sorry if
you felt that way this week. I'm not making excuses—
promise—but please remember that I've been the one left
out so many times before. How many times have I come out
in the yard to talk, and you or Jackson would ask the other
to do something, then give me those "sorry" smiles? What
did I do? I held my hurt in and left. It isn't in me to
express to you or anyone else when I have my feelings
hurt. I'm telling you this now only because I want you to
know that I understand how you might feel and I want to
say that you—and you alone—are the person I completely
trust. I haven't reached that point with anyone else in my
life. I've always had only you & I guess this is right because
I think I'm meant to keep to myself.

The only things in my life that I have *ever* kept from you have had to do with Jackson. This is right I think, because I want Jackson to be my boyfriend, not my friend. I love *you*, Tommy, with every single fiber in my being, maybe more than I could feel for a lover, if that makes sense.

Right now, God seems to be putting his hand into my heaped up heart and trying to put things in order. I'm sorry if some things—like this apology—have happened later than they should have.

I love you,

Maggie

June 5

At night I lie in bed and try to connect the dots in the ceiling tiles. Sometimes I see faces, but mostly I see ducks. Mary's engagement picture was in the newspaper with an article about her announcement tea. It said, "From her trousseau, Miss Sartor chose a long, beige cotton frock." If I ever get married, I'm definitely going to elope.

June 6

Note on the back door when I woke up:

No sad songs; no, none at all. That would really be silly. I'm happy. I'm going now, to pray by the sea. Love, Jackson Bye. I love you. O.K.? O.K.

A bunch of us were at Jackson's house to say good-bye this morning. Everyone else was sad, but I was positively joyful! I'm ready for my life to feel normal. Tonight Dash and I went out, but he got mad at me because I didn't want to drink or go parking. Just couldn't deal with it. I can not get clear in my mind what I'm supposed to do. Stella came in from New Orleans today.

June 7

Went out with Dash and he said he has quit drinking. Stella was upset tonight. I love my family and I wish there were more ways I could show it. Jackson is too far away.

June 8

> (for J.B.)
> He's not here but I'm far gone,
> I fear my Love will leave and I will last
> Much longer than his need for me.

June 9

Lately in my dreams, I am always trying to run, but my legs will only move in slow motion. Twice I dreamed my teeth fell out.

June 10

The only thing I get upset about is my family. I wish there weren't so much fighting between us. The whole house is so sad. So tired. Dash told me he loved me again.

June 11

Dash called twice. I'm thinking of Jackson too much. I've lost all incentive to do anything. Tonight I was going through Great-Grandma Beulah's Bible and the letters she saved. There is one postcard sent from Paris that says: "There is always someone somewhere who is watching you, thinking of you, breathing love across the silent waves. My heart works harder and grows sadder each day."

June 12

I have to find within myself the shape of my life, my true dimensions. When I know my limits, then I will be able to handle things.

June 13

How do I explain to my parents that there is *so much* I want to do in my life and this is a really awkward time for me to put my life on hold?

June 14

Dash called tonight and he got mad when he found out I went out with Tony. We decided we're only going to date each other. I hope this is the right thing. I'm tired of dating around. I wrote Jackson.

June 15

School is out and it's harder for Bill to stay out of trouble.

June 16

No one has time for anyone else. Mama is really starting to show.

June 18

I've been getting letters from Jackson *every* day for three days. The letter I got today is four pages long, but at the end he wrote, "Don't write too much if you don't want to."

June 20

I want my family to be happy again.

June 21

The wedding was perfect and Mary was perfect. She was a beautiful bride. My knee's bugging me. I know I should feel more thoughtful about all of this, but my heart's not in it. Mary is gone and I should have paid more attention, because now I've lost my chance. Jackson called from Miami & every now and then I realize how much I miss him. Then I *miss* him.

(later) I don't know why I didn't write this down before, but tonight on the phone, Jackson said "I love you" to me for the first time.

June 23

I don't want to become too attached to Dash. He has a one-track mind about sex & can seem shallow in that way.

June 24

Volunteered at a day camp for retarded children today and enjoyed it. Tonight Dash called and *told* me to come over. First, he asked me to tell him I loved him & I couldn't because I don't. Then we had a disagreement because he wants to go further (sex wise) and I'm not going to do it. It really bothers him. He's not used to it, I guess. I'm not terribly distressed. I told him "no matter how much I care for you, I'm not going to change for you." He said he'd thought of that.

June 27

Dash called to talk but I couldn't say what he wanted to hear, so it didn't end well.

June 29

I'm just going to let the Dash problem find its own solution because I don't have the energy or inclination to force it anywhere.

June 30

Letter from Jackson: "I'm getting a good tan & wild sun-bleached hair. I want to forget about you & then when I do I feel guilty for not thinking about you. All my love to you, Margaret Sartor—whoever in this world you are; whatever in this world you are. Run Baby run. You are so beautiful to me. Weird but true."

Jackson has swallowed my heart.

July 1
I broke up with Dash. He lied to me about a girl he was with & I have too much pride to put up with that. When I said I was through with him, all he could say was that he would ruin me anyway, and that I'm "too nice." But he underestimates me. I can handle Dash. I just can't handle being lied to.

July 2
Wrote to Jackson that I broke it off with Dash.

July 4
Drove to Alto this morning with Daddy and we ran into a man who wanted to talk. Later Daddy said, "Mr. Bud dipped a little too deep in the bottle today." Mr. Bud said that when he and Daddy were boys, someone dug a well and discovered natural gas under Alto. But before the well was capped, someone (no one knows still) threw a match in it and it exploded and the well burned for two years. There's still a crater where it was, but it's filled with water, and it's so deep they've never been able to find the bottom. Mr. Bud said that if they'd capped that gas well sooner, we'd all be rich.

July 7
Got a telegram from Jackson. Right now I'm on a Trailways bus with all the Bengal Belles headed for drill team camp in Dallas for a week. Jackson will be home soon. I wonder what that will be like.

July 13

Back home. The Kilgore Rangerettes, who ran the camp, were great, except one Rangerette who was a pill. We went to dance classes all day, worked hard, and ate like pigs. One night Pam and I mooned some boys out the dorm window. Another night we ambushed Hallie and covered her with toothpaste when she came out of the shower. We placed fourth in the final competition and I figure we did fine, but some people were upset. Dash called me in Dallas and said he missed me. We went out tonight.

July 14

At camp, Clarissa told me something. She said it makes her nervous to come to a white neighborhood. That surprised me. Clarissa also said when I talk about boys, I remind her of Scarlett from *Gone with the Wind*.

July 15

Dash wants us to be together. We still fight. Nothing is settled.

July 16

Clothilde says Dash has the goo goo with the eyes. She sounds like Flip Wilson.

July 17

Ate crawfish at Dash's house but I made him take me home early. I've decided one thing: Dating is for the birds. It's too demanding.

July 18

Went to the mall with Angela and some greaser guys followed us through the parking lot. We were scared to death.

July 20

Aunt Ida came by today & she talked about my cousin Mary Jo who lives in Atlanta. She said MJ didn't much like Atlanta when she first got there. The only other place she'd ever lived was Pasadena, Texas, and the people there were like here. Aunt Ida said that when MJ went to Pasadena, the church there put her right to work & she was happy. In Atlanta, she went to church three straight Sundays & every single time, the preacher introduced himself & forgot he'd met her. So now Mary Jo stays home on Sundays & watches church on TV.

July 21

Dash called & we fought. He hung up mad. So be it.

July 22

Finished Anne Frank's diary and cried for a long time. She lived with such fear and during a terrible time in the world, but still she was just a girl trying to figure herself out and get along with people.

July 25

There was an article in the paper about Great-Aunt Julia, who is a painter. In it, she said it was her daughter Beth that got her to start painting. Aunt Beth was a doctor and she died years ago so I never knew her. Aunt Julia is sort of famous for her paintings but now she mostly does needlepoint.

July 26

I don't want to fight with anyone but I seem to fight with everybody.

July 27

Ate supper at Dash's house. I trust him more & he is much more careful with me now. Sex is less of an issue/conflict. I can tell that he enjoys being with me.

July 28

Betsy invited me to a new church that meets in a trailer off I-20. She called it "Beth Annie Church" but when we got there the sign said *Bethany* Church. People were dancing in the aisles and speaking in tongues and the Spirit was MOVING!

July 29

Dash and I have grown close these past months. But Jackson is coming home tomorrow. It's fair to say that I'm romantically attached to Dash, but my heart is still bound to Jackson. (Tommy says Dash is handsome, but I'll "grow out of it.")

July 30

Jackson is home. Tommy and I went out to meet him at the airport. It was a bit anticlimactic for some reason I can't figure out exactly. Then this afternoon he came looking for me, and tonight we went to dinner at the nicest steak house in town. He was telling me stories about his summer and I was so happy and he was so happy. Afterward we went to the end of a dead-end road to be together, but it was awkward. Why was it? Suddenly we heard a car driving up & people laughing & calling. "Maggie! Jackson! Maggie!" It was Tommy and Betsy with an ice cream pie. (Didn't tell Jackson I've been seeing Dash again.)

July 31

Jackson and Tommy put on a Bengal *Beaux* show. They rolled up their shorts and put on lipstick and rouge and did high kicks! They were good at it! I was laughing so hard I was saying "Stop . . . stop!" because I couldn't breathe. Later, Jackson and I ate dinner at the Holiday Grill and Dash walked in but I didn't say anything to him.

August 1
Dash called and was upset I didn't show up at his ball game. Jackson just happened to come over while I was on the phone and he heard me arguing. Since Jackson thought I had broken things off with Dash, he's confused. (So am I.) Jackson unhinges my good sense and now I've hurt *all* of us.

August 3
Jackson called long-distance to say he was in Dallas with his good friend Yvonne. I felt so weak & heavy.

August 4
I don't feel too good. BB practice has started up again and I feel out of shape. We get weighed in every morning before practice. I put on a couple of pounds since camp. One girl put on eight pounds and the choreographer yelled at her.

August 6
Mary is in town. She told me I should quit Bengal Belles because it takes up too much time. She said, "What's more important to you?" I almost hated her when she said that.

August 8
I rode my bike to Coach Baylor's auto parts store, but he wasn't there. Got thirsty and went into a diner called Irene's to get a Coke. A lady (Irene) asked me my name and then said, "You're Dr. Tom's daughter?" When I said I was, she said, "Why, you're just a rich girl playing over here in colored town." That *shocked* me. She could tell it did, because then she said she was only kidding, and that she had a daughter that liked to do different things now & then, too.

August 10

The new plan around the old homestead is for me to move out of my bedroom so the baby can have it. It's fine really. I'm getting my own phone line.

August 11

Tommy and I were sitting in the den looking at Mama's new book on paintings by Georgia O'Keeffe. I said some of them were spiritual and made me think of God. Tommy said some of them *were* spiritual, but they made him think of penises and vaginas.

August 12

I am sixteen years old. I am not sweet. Momma Doll said some girls get married at sixteen. She gave me a typewriter.

August 13

A letter came from a girl who worked with Jackson in Dominica. She said they were good friends and everyone there knew about me and that my nickname was Sister Golden Hair. Tommy thinks I should write her back, but what's the point? Went out with (handsome) Dash tonight.

August 14

Last year I stole a book of poems by Emily Dickinson from the school library and I can't bring myself to take it back. I can't imagine not having it. I need it. I think it needs me.

August 15

Tonight was our *first* Bengal Belle halftime performance. We sat in the stands in our white gloves and boots and our black capes covering our uniforms for the first quarter of the game. Second quarter we warmed up under the stands. At halftime, we removed our capes and put our hands on our hips and walked in a line out to the edge of the field. When the band was in place, we marched out and lined up horizontally across the fifty-yard line, facing the crowd. There were a couple of seconds of silence (*so* exciting) and then Betsy blew her whistle. The band started playing and we danced and did our high kicks. Afterward, the crowd applauded and we took a bow in unison and marched off the field while they were still clapping. I *loved* it!!

August 17
Today the pastor at Bethany Baptist pointed & asked me to rise & prophesied that I would be a lamp for Jesus. I've lost 6 lbs.

August 18
Dash and I mess around, but I get the feeling he's afraid to touch me. I think that means my personality means more to him than sex.

August 19
Practically everyone in town went to the school board meeting tonight and there was a lot of yelling. Why is it so hard for people to get along?

August 20
Mama says desegregation is like the blind men and the elephant. People only understand the little piece of it that touches their lives, but they *think* they know what the whole damn elephant looks like.

August 22
I'm an unreasonable person. I've prayed to God to change me, but I don't think I'm changing.

August 23

What is it between me and Jackson . . . is it a secret?

August 24

My muscles are SO SORE. —— I'm talking to Dash right now on the phone. He made me laugh! Well, he's gone. I wish he'd call back. I don't know. I'm glad he called.

August 25

Tommy dreamed that we were getting married, and in the dream his mother was furious, but we were very excited about our presents.

August 27

The new principal at Monroe High is a big-game hunter and has the heads of dead animals all over his office. There is a front half of a bear coming out of the wall above the secretary's desk. A man in Arkansas blew up his wife with a stick of dynamite while she was in bed with another man.

August 28

Tony asked me out for next weekend, so it's starting up again. It's against Mama's rules to say no to a boy if I don't have a good reason, and I don't know how to explain my reasons.

August 29

There was a dance at the school after the Jamboree and I went stag with Angela. I tried to talk to Dash but he walked away—which made me so mad that I danced the whole night right where he could see him.

August 30

Dash called & we had it out on the phone & then we went out & talked some more. He says he really cares, but that if we were going steady, he wouldn't be satisfied sexually & that he'd cheat on me—so I don't know what I should do. I feel as though I'd be protected with Dash even though there'd be complications. I do care for him. He said he would try again if I asked him to. Even if I'm not in love with Dash, he feels safe to me.

August 31
I can run. It's patience I lack.

September 1
I seem to continually let down the people that matter the most to me.

September 5
The bus trip to Lafayette was long but I sat with Angela and we had pillows and chips and dip and played cards and it was fun. Then we won the game and the bus ride back was long and tedious. Dash was waiting at the bus (at 2:00 a.m.) to pick me up. The players got back before us and had time to shower and everything. He *smelled* so good. It felt *good* to be near him.

September 6
Went out with Tony and the *whole* time he bugged me about Dash but I asked him to go to church with me tomorrow and I was surprised that he said yes.

September 7
Tony called and said his car wouldn't start, so I went to church with my parents.

September 8
I didn't sit by Tony in study hall today. He acted teed off, but he knows there can't be anything serious between us?

September 12

Tony has started calling me "Valentine."

September 13

Strange week. This week was rough. Dash had a date with someone else after the game & I went home alone. After he took her home, he called me. . . . So, we're going steady. I let him touch me and I didn't feel wrong about it. I don't want to have a relationship based on sex, but I want this relationship. Besides, I know this is mostly superficial and Dash cares about me. I'm happy. God is still on my mind every minute.

September 14

Rode my bike over to the 6:30 a.m. Mass at Jesus Good Shepherd this morning. I liked it. I went to school in a decent mood.

September 15

Dash and I are together but I don't want everyone to know right away. I'd just rather it not be a public announcement. It's kind of like Nixon and Vietnam—the ground war is over, but I'm keeping my boats at sea.

September 16

I think I committed a sin today. Cynthia was reading her Bible in the hallway and a crowd of seniors was nearby and Dash made fun of her and I didn't say anything. I'm ashamed.

September 20

Old Mr. Dyer died and his son Billy Dyer came to the funeral. No one has seen or heard from Billy in twenty-one years and there he was. After the funeral, Billy went out to the house and stood around talking about fishing and hunting with the men, and then he left not saying if he would ever come back. Everyone was *dying* to know what it was that happened twenty-one years ago, but Mr. Dyer never did tell anybody.

September 21
Dash doesn't want me to jog on the track with the football players after Bengal Belle practice, but Coach Smith likes it because he says it motivates the players. I like it because I can outrun half the team (the fat half). I see no good reason to stop.

September 22
I got Tony to tell me why he calls me "Valentine" (now some other boys are doing it too) and it's because my ass looks like an upside-down heart. I told him that's OK as long as he doesn't mind me calling him *Breadloaf Butt.*

September 26
Tonight was the biggest football game in Monroe High history! (Almost 10,000 people were there!) We won and Dash was so high! He was the star!! We had a great time after the game—at least until the end of the evening when we were alone parking, and then it got uncomfortable.

September 27
I have to admit it's gotten a little weird. Dash has begun to drink more, to cuss more, & he wants *more* from me. He said something cruel to me today. I don't know how to face my life.

September 28
I get very jealous when Dash flirts with other girls in front of me. Why?

September 29
I'm beginning to believe that falling in love is like playing Blind Man's Bluff and whoever you touch is IT.

October 1
No needs. No feelings.

October 3
I'm extremely worried about my mother and my father and their baby. But I weigh 109, and basically I'm doing great.

October 6
I'm so depressed.

October 7
My life and my family are about to change forever.

October 8
I've been going to Mass at Jesus Good Shepherd for weeks and to-day Maria Hayes told me I'm not supposed to take communion there unless I'm Catholic. She told me that Catholics believe that when you take communion, the wine and bread *literally* turn into the blood and flesh of Jesus. When I told that to my mother, she didn't believe me. She said, "Well, how do they explain that the taste doesn't change?"

October 12
The football team picked me to be Maid of Honor for Homecoming! Dash came and told me in front of all my friends at BB practice (which was awkward) and I was very surprised! It's an honor. Dash is in heaven. I'm a little worried what my friends think.

October 13

We had our picture taken for the paper this morning. I went shopping after school by myself because all my friends were in BB practice and Mama wasn't up to it.

October 14

Mrs. Dilworth, who has been the Homecoming coordinator for the last century, showed us how to sit properly during the game. We had to *practice* it. It boils down to never crossing your legs and imagining that you are wearing a back brace.

October 15

Jackson is coming in town for Homecoming weekend. He wants to see me, but I don't think that would be right. Jackson wrote, "Don't let it all mess things up. I never meant to fence you in." (But he *didn't*. I fenced myself in.)

October 16

The parade this afternoon was fine except that it was humid so I wore my hair in a bun. Edgar Napoleon drove me in his dad's Cadillac convertible. I had no idea what the other girls were going to wear (they're all cheerleaders) and it turned out they *all* looked like Charlie's Angels. My dress had long sleeves and a high collar and I looked like one of the Waltons.

October 17

Homecoming was great & now it's over. After the game, Dash & I drank too much & we got carried away and I'm not sure it's right for me. I don't feel wrong about it, but I'd like the relationship to move in a different direction.

October 20

I worry that so much has been going my way in school that I'll become dependent on honors & grades to feel good about myself.

November 2

Uncle Charlie had a heart attack and is in the hospital. He's OK, but Mama said he woke up and pulled the feeding tube out of his throat, and didn't know where he was, so now they have him strapped down. She made a big sign to put by his bed:

CHARLIE LAWTON!
YOU ARE IN ST. FRANCIS <u>HOSPITAL.</u>
YOU HAVE HAD HEART SURGERY.
IF YOU <u>BEHAVE</u> YOU WILL GET BETTER.

November 3

Uncle Charlie is fine. He doesn't remember any of what happened over the last few days. Mama is relieved.

November 7

I feel like I'm living in a place where I run into my family by accident. Bill says he feels the same way but that it doesn't bother him.

November 9

I know I can't use my family problems as an excuse, but being unhappy at home makes it harder for me to figure out *anything*. Dash & I have experimented with sex & I feel I have kept it under control but it's not so fun for me anymore.

November 10

Jackson and I talked on the phone tonight. I'm so *grateful* for his friendship. I only hope Mama's baby brings my family back together.

November 11

I want to be open with people, but I find that very difficult to do.

November 12

I can't complain . . . but it seems things have gone downhill & I know it. I'm in a fog. I'm not sure of Jackson's place in my life but the bond is still there. I worry about my mother all the time. Bill is having problems.

November 13

Lust is the wrong basis for a relationship. Why can't I admit this to myself and move on? I see very clearly the drawbacks in continuing my relationship with Dash.

November 15

Tonight Jackson called long-distance. When Dash showed up, I wouldn't get off the phone. Dash blew up and I got off the phone. Then we blew up and broke up.

November 16

I'm happy. I feel much more free.

November 18

Hallie came over. She told me she envies me because I don't change who I am to be more popular. She started crying and told me how unhappy she was. But her unhappiness boils down to fears that she'll never have *money* to do the things she wants and that she's not beautiful enough to *get* what she wants. I didn't know what to say. Our job on earth, as I see it, is to hold on through the hard parts and to try to be a good person.

November 19
In the letter I got today, Jackson wrote that he gets very lonely at college and wants to come home. I could lean on Jackson right now, and I'd like to, but I feel I have to be careful with both our hearts.

November 20
Daddy expects Bill to become a doctor, but I don't know what he expects of me—maybe to marry a doctor?

November 22
I'm seeing Mitch Hardy again. He keeps calling. I don't trust it for a minute.

November 23
I've had a couple of dates with Mitch. But he's dating other girls too.

November 25
Ellen says she never felt more beautiful than when she was pregnant. Mother says that some women love being pregnant, but she is not one of them.

December 1
The doctors have decided to put Mama in the hospital *tomorrow* and induce labor. That way there will be more safety and more control. Daddy says Bill and I both have to go to school. I'm very worried. I'm praying and praying that Mama will be fine and the baby will be fine and we'll all be fine.

December 2

I did go to school this morning, but I couldn't stand it, so at lunchtime I got Mitch to take me to the hospital. When I got to the waiting room, Momma Doll, Aunt Lou, and Ellen were there. Mama came down the hall on a gurney and she tried to smile at me but she looked terrible. Her knees were bent & her legs apart under a sheet. Daddy had his hand at her side & was walking next to her. He never looked up. She was so pale, she was almost totally white. Aunt Lou said the doctors predicted a long labor, but two hours later Uncle Henry walked into the waiting area with a grin on his face and said to me, "Did you want a little brother or a little sister?" I said a little brother. He said, "Well, you have a little sister." Then everyone started crowding around Uncle Henry and asking questions and I was completely confused. Daddy came out and he was all smiles and said, "Your mother is fine. Your sister is fine."—It's all over. I'm so relieved I almost don't feel *anything.*

December 3

I had to go to school today, but everyone there was so thrilled! I had no idea. They announced the baby in Student Council meeting and everyone clapped. After school, I went to the hospital to see the baby and talk to Mama. The baby is kind of homely. She has a full head of dark hair and her eyes are gray-blue. Mama asked what I wanted to name her and I said Emily Christine Sartor.

December 4

My parents named the baby Sara Wooding Sartor.

December 9

Letter from Jackson: "Life goes on, and things change; we all need room to move ahead. If we didn't, we'd be prisoners of our own lives."—It's *right* that Jackson pulls away from me. I have nothing to offer him.

December 13
Tommy & I sat out on his patio and talked for an hour or so tonight. I had the feeling a couple of times that he wanted to tell me something but he didn't.

December 15
Mama hired a maid, Eloise, to help out with Sara. Eloise is *huge* but she is nice to be around.

December 17
Mitch and I are pretty tight, but he's also been dating Bonnie *Hell* and the situation has gotten kind of ugly.

December 18
Bonnie Dell is gorgeous and she's MEAN and she is really getting on my nerves.

December 19
We trimmed the Christmas tree. When we hung up stockings, we didn't have one for Sara, so Bill hung up one of her teeny tiny socks on the mantel with a tack. We were happy.

December 20
Daddy and I and Bill took gifts out to the Baptist Children's Home, where the orphans live. It was dark and the buildings are right in the middle of a huge pecan grove. It was eerie.

December 24
God is my only real lover. Please let me sleep deep & awake early.

December 26

I'm working at the KNOE-TV station over the holidays (for free) and doing anything they can find for me to do. Tonight I floor-directed the first half of the "Mr. Wonder's Children's Show."

December 28

Mitch won't leave me alone. I'm kind of dying inside.

December 30

Mitch had a date with Bonnie Dell tonight and called me after and that's when I broke it off entirely. I don't need to deal with that kind of deception. It made me feel sick. But then Mitch wouldn't let it go and said he loved me. I kept saying "no" and he kept saying "yes" and in the end I guess he talked me into dating him. But I'm not good at relationships—I *told* him that.

December 31

I'm sort of drunk, but not too much. I brought a plastic champagne glass back from a party because I read in a book that the perfect breast was the shape of the inside of a champagne glass. And guess what? I'm perfect! I am Miss American Pie! BYE BYE 1975! WHAT A YEAR!

1976

"Bury My Heart at Wounded Knee"

January 5
Too much feeling and no words.

January 10
I think human desire may be the enemy of spirituality.

January 11
It's not just my need of romantic companionship, it's also my need for love from my parents that overwhelms me.

January 12
Found a dead cardinal on the patio, and thought that if I only saw a red bird once in a blue moon, it would seem like a miracle.

January 13
Mama is so tired that she's afraid she'll fall asleep and drop Sara when she's feeding her at night.

January 14
Life goes on—but lately it feels off.

January 15
Taking care of Sara makes my heart race for fear I'll do something wrong.

January 16
Everyone else in the neighborhood throws their poinsettias in the trash, but Mama puts them out by the road so they'll get picked up and taken home by somebody. She calls this "the baby in the bulrushes" solution.

January 17

Everything I do, I do so my family will be proud of me. I can't explain how important this is to me.

January 18

I wish I could communicate with my father more. Sometimes I'm afraid of him.

January 19

I'm spending a lot of time with Mitch. Mama is very tired.

January 20

I WANT TO HAVE A HAPPY NORMAL LIFE. I WANT MY FAMILY TO *BE* A FAMILY.

January 24

It sort of crept up on me, but I'm really attached to Mitch. This is where my problems start.

January 26

I would give Mitch up (I mean it!) if it wasn't the right thing, but it would be hard.

January 27

My love and faith in God is the most certain pleasure of my life.

January 28

This morning I was unnerved by Mitch. I can't *stand* to be compared to anyone! I think I have a complex about others being better than me. I WILL NOT CHANGE MYSELF TO SUIT SOMEONE ELSE.

January 30
Sometimes love is the enemy.

February 1
Mama says that sleep is the good friend who never returns her calls.

February 2
Mitch called and we both got mad and jealous of Dash and Bonnie Dell and were accusing each other of stuff. I don't like how I feel.

February 3
Today I came home from school early and slept from 11:30 a.m. to 6 p.m. Sometimes I just want to take all the boys in my school and fry them in deep fat.

February 4
Betsy thinks it's unnatural for blacks and whites to date because God would have made us all the same race if he intended us to intermarry. I love Betsy, but I don't know where she gets some of her ideas.

February 5
Mama has to put on her reading glasses to button up Sara's clothes or clip Sara's fingernails. She squints and moves Sara back and forth like she's trying to read the ingredients on a cereal box.

February 6
I'm trying to enjoy Mitch. I want to make it work. I *told* him so.

February 7
Mitch says I need to learn some things, like:

1. How to distinguish between *talking* and *flirting* when speaking with any boy besides him.
2. How *not* to overreact to good *or* bad news.
3. When to say a game was *good*, and when to say *nothing at all*, in reference to any and all sports from golf to football.

I told him my personality is not up for a total renovation, just a tune-up.

February 8
When I was a girl, a scraggly-haired tomboy of a girl, I thought like a scraggly-haired tomboy of a girl, and acted like a bitch. Now that I am a teenager, I have brushed my hair, added highlights, and tried to stop my bitchy ways.

February 9
Bill came home *wasted* tonight. Mama & Daddy made him walk a straight line at the foot of their bed, and he managed to do it . . . then he walked into the hallway and threw up. Daddy was *furious*, but not about his being drunk. He kept pointing his finger at Bill and saying, "You *lied* to me, son. *Never* lie to me!"

February 10
Things are not so good.

February 11
I'm living in the twilight zone. Yesterday I found out that Bonnie Dell might be pregnant, and if she *is* pregnant, Mitch is the father. When I heard this, I got upset. Because I needed to hear Mitch say it to my face, I took the car without asking. Then Mama got upset. Now I'm grounded (for taking the car) and my parents

know about everything. Mitch says he was only having sex with Bonnie Dell because he couldn't have sex with me, and so he reasons this is partly *my* fault. Even Bonnie Dell wants to put some of the blame on me. The way I see it, they made their choices and I made mine, and I don't want to talk about it anymore.

February 12
Right now my life is a twisted version of *Gone with the Wind*, and everyone thinks I'm Melanie . . . but I'm really a retarded Scarlett O'Hara.

February 13
I want to *rid* myself of all the jealousy, envy, short temper, impatience, selfishness & turbulence I've been feeling lately.

February 14
Tony gave me a homemade valentine. It was very sweet. It was a folded, stapled index card, with my name spelled wrong on the outside, and inside it said, "*I* didn't forget you, Sweetheart." (Mitch sent me a box of chocolates that I threw in the trash, after I gave some to the dogs.)

February 15
I wish I could surround myself with quiet and impose that quiet on everyone else.

February 16
Why do I miss Mitch?

February 17
Stella is seeing a psychiatrist. Bonnie Dell is not pregnant.

February 18
Mama says Stella is seeing a psychiatrist because it will help her feel better about herself. I hope it does.

February 19
I know Mama & Daddy wish I would talk to them more, but that's just too hard for me.

February 20
Mama told me a story while we were cleaning up the kitchen. When I was around two years old and Stella was seven, one night Mama was washing Stella's hair in the bath tub and had stripped down to her slip and panties. I started beating on the door and crying, and she was yelling "I'll be out in a minute!" But I wouldn't stop crying, so she started screaming for Daddy, "Tom, Tom, come get Margaret!" He didn't come, so she opened the door and stomped into the den, still in her wet slip, saying, "TOM! Couldn't you hear me?" and there was Daddy sitting quietly with this older doctor who had stopped by to have a little chat about Daddy's future plans. Mama said, "Oh, don't mind me, I'm just bathing the children." She walked out and Daddy never mentioned it.

February 22
It's to that point again where I'm bored, but my jealousy of Bonnie Dell complicates my feelings. Mitch talks about us getting married and I don't know why I let him. Or I do know, and it scares me because I'm afraid I'll do something I'll regret.

February 24
I have a routine to get to sleep. Read, pee, lights out, close eyes, pray, sleep. If anything interrupts me, I have to start all over again (from the peeing) in order to relax. Sometimes I hum while I pee.

The whole thing is somewhat irritating and I'm pretty sure it's not normal.

February 25
I try to avoid Bonnie Dell, but I'm not going to let her confine my life.

February 26
I'm glad Mitch isn't jealous of Tommy. Tommy says about Mitch, "He's a nice guy. Just don't marry him."

February 27
I smoke cigarettes. (Not a lot, but sometimes.) I steal them from Daddy's dresser or from Stella's purse when she's home. Smoking relaxes me. I can see how the peace pipe was a great idea.

February 28
When I flip the switch on the kitchen disposal and see the leftovers and soapy water get sucked down, I get this weird *urge* to stick my hand in. So I tell myself: DON'T think that! It might come true! And I turn it off. Washing food down the disposal is like standing at the edge of a cliff—which naturally makes you think about jumping off.

March 1
I feel a certain warmth (love?) for Mitch, but any normal girl at sixteen years old would be thinking of marriage & such, so I don't know what's wrong with me.

March 5
Aunt Georgia was here and she kept asking me about Mitch and if I was going to LSU with him. She said when you're in love, you

should work around it because love is hard to find. I find it difficult to believe that love is so hard to find.

March 6
Today in the kitchen, Mama told me about Kegel (Kagle?) exercises, which women do for the muscles around the vagina (and it's especially important to do them after having a baby). I asked her when she does them and she said, "Oh, whenever I am sitting with nothing to do, like in church."

March 7
The crazy part of my mind is like a mischievous pet that I have to keep watch over or it might behave badly while I'm not paying attention.

March 8
Stella feels so bad that she assumes everyone else feels better. But she's wrong.

March 9
I think only God can fill the dark holes of who we are.

March 10
When I try to do the vagina exercises, it gives me the *shivers.*

March 11
I was reading my book in the den tonight and out of the blue, Daddy asked if I was doing OK. I said I was fine. Then I came in my room & fell to pieces.

March 12
Mitch is cruel to me in small ways, but usually I'm glad he's my boyfriend.

March 13
Daddy told me about his Uncle Jim. He said Uncle Jim had a reputation for shooting the bull. Uncle Jim was a farmer, but on Mondays and Wednesdays he mostly hung around the Sartor Bros. Store talking to customers. On Tuesdays and Thursdays, he drove to Rayville and hung around the barber shop. On Friday and Saturday he showed up at the Harper Drug Store in Mangum, and on Sundays he farmed, so he didn't have to go to church.

March 15
Tommy snuck over to my house late last night and before he knocked on my window, he said he saw a silhouette of me on the curtains, sitting in a chair reading a book. I thought that was nice. He said he liked it, too. Tommy says he can't *wait* to graduate from high school (he'll be done in two months!) . . . that got me thinking . . . what am I going to do next year when I'm a senior and Tommy is gone?!

March 16
An odd thing: my feelings for Jackson are so deep that they are more a *fact* of my life, than an *urge*.

March 18
I have to believe it's possible to have turmoil without, but peace within.

March 19
I think Emily Dickinson cut herself off from the world because that was the only way she could have a spiritual life that wasn't distorted by other people's expectations of her.

March 20

I read a story about a fish (Colancath?) that scientists thought had been extinct for 80 million years, and then a fisherman caught one off the coast of Africa—which proves there are secrets *everywhere*.

March 21

After church, Mama asked me to go with her to visit Miss Inez at the Old Folks' Home. It was horrible! When we got there, Miss Inez was dressed and sitting on her bed. An aide came in to change the sheets just as we arrived. Miss Inez said hello to Mama, but didn't recognize me. She asked us to have breakfast with her, but the aide said she'd had breakfast and so Miss Inez started arguing with her.

"No, I haven't."

"Yes you did, Honey. You had plenty."

Mama suggested we go out on the porch and sit and Miss Inez said "OK, let me get my purse." But the aide picked up the purse and opened it up and began taking things out. She took out a tube of toothpaste, 3 pairs of panties, and a pint (opened) of whole milk. Miss Inez said, "Wait a minute! What are you doing? I need that!" and grabbed the purse back and stuffed her underwear back in. The aide took the purse and pulled the underwear out. Miss Inez sat back on the bed and let out a big sigh. I felt *so* sorry for her. Then the aide looked at us and said, "Don't you worry. She's just got to *adjust*."

I feel sick.

March 24

What will happen if one day the wrong side of my brain wins?

March 25

When Jesus tried to explain to the Jews why they didn't understand what he was saying, he said, "He who is of God, hears God's words:

you do not hear them, because you are not of God."—I think he was saying that what you *hear* depends on who you *are*.

March 26
Thought: Jesus had an ability to confound the mighty. Peace is a kind of power.

March 27
Just before dark, I was walking on the levee, and as I passed one backyard I saw an elderly man walking around his patio in a red robe and gray pajamas looking for something. He was whistling. Then a young Doberman puppy came bounding around the side of the house, wagging his entire rear end. The two of them climbed into a metal chaise with green cushions and the old man began whistling a tune, and not too badly. It took me a minute to recognize, but he was whistling "Swing low, sweet chariot, coming for to carry me home . . ."

March 30
Mitch is running for president of the senior class, and he's pressuring me to try out for varsity cheerleader, but it's not what I want. What I want is not to dread my life.

April 3
Every night I think of all the stupid things I have ever done in my whole life, and that's why I can't get to sleep. Dash called tonight. He asked me to marry him.

April 4
The deadline for cheerleader tryouts was today, and I didn't turn in my name. Mitch is upset, but I know I'm right.

April 16

At the dance tonight Mitch yelled at me in front of people and I started crying! I'm not up to this anymore. I'd rather be alone.

April 21

I've gained five pounds! I've been eating too much & too much of anything is a bad thing, maybe even a sin. I'm beginning to grasp something about myself . . . I'm a terrible girlfriend.

April 23

Stella is still having trouble. My parents don't know how to help her.

April 24

I can't seem to give what love wants to take.

April 25

I don't expect to be outrageously happy, but I do hope one day to feel content.

April 26

I love watching Daddy play with Sara. I remember exactly how it felt to hold Daddy's hand when I was little. You could show me the hands of a thousand men and I could pick out my Daddy's, no problem.

April 27

Ellen told me and Tommy the story of his older brother Evan running away from home when he was seventeen, and she had us in hysterics! Evan's girlfriend Melissa called Ellen one night and said, in this real itty bitty voice which Ellen mimicked,

"Mrs. Townsend, I wasn't supposed to call you until tomorrow but I'm soooooo worried I just haaaaaad to call."

"What is it, Melissa?" (Ellen didn't particularly like Melissa.)

"I'm calling to tell you Evan ran away from home."

"Oh Melissa, don't be silly."

"He told me to tell you to look in the second drawer of your white bedroom dresser."

"Oh . . . Really?" (Ellen paused.) "Can you hold?"

So Ellen goes to her dresser and finds a sealed envelope with "Mama" written on the outside and she picks up the phone and says, "Thanks for calling, Melissa. Bye," and hangs up. In the note, Evan asked Ellen not to call the police because he would be back in a week. He took her car & her gas card & he was with his best friend, Doodle Bug Newton, & they were on their way to Pike's Peak. They made it to Pike's Peak eating only peanut butter and jelly sandwiches the whole way, but by the time they got there, they didn't have enough money to buy tickets to ride to the top, so they had to turn around and drive straight home.

May 1

I should probably marry Tommy.

May 2

> *In this short life*
> *That only lasts an hour,*
> *How much, how little,*
> *Is within our power?*
> —by Emily Dickinson

May 3

Mama & Daddy don't understand me, so I wrote them a letter. They just don't see me as I truly *am*—a sixteen-year-old girl *fighting* to learn how to live!

May 4

(2:12 a.m.) When I was in third grade, my parents started letting me ride my bike to school. I was supposed to *walk* my bike across Loop Road, but one day I got to the intersection and there was a break in the cars, so instead of stopping, I stood up on my pedals and gunned it. The road was wet. The handle bars twisted. My bike turned sideways, skidded, and suddenly I was under it. My books scattered everywhere. Cars stopped in both directions. One mother got *out* of her stopped car to help me. The kids in the cars were looking at me. My life was over. I was so embarrassed I couldn't sleep for a week. I'm STILL embarrassed. That's why I'm awake.

May 5

Daddy wrote me back.

Dear Margaret—

I have just been re-reading your letter. I appreciate your expressing your worries and concerns so truthfully.

Please let your mind be at ease because your Mother and I are extremely proud of your accomplishments and your attitude and ability to be your own person. I'm sure that we don't express this to you often enough—but we feel it just the same. I think that you have a maturity of judgment beyond your years, but still I think it is my duty sometimes to censor your activities based on my somewhat longer & broader experience.

I know that the social scene these days tends to go overboard with boy–girl relationships, but there is great strength in righteousness in all situations and if you are right—the others know it in their hearts and can not help

but respect and like you more for it in the last analysis.
Don't ever think you need to apologize for doing what is
right.

We have enjoyed your poetry when you have shared it
with us—I think it is great to have the gift of expressing not
only facts but feelings in words and writings—something I
have never had—but it doesn't mean the feelings aren't
there.

We are very proud of our daughter and I am confident
that you are on the road to a good and complete life—We
can only try to provide the opportunity and perhaps
some example—the rest is up to you and you are doing a
fine job.

Love, Daddy

May 7

I know that I'll never lead the life I want with Mitch.

May 8

Walking down the hallway with Tony, I made a crack about my
frizzy hair & noisy clogs and he said, "Girl, you have style. I don't
know anyone else like you."

May 10

Seniors finished tests last week and today they were all gone. No
Tommy. I felt so on my own.

May 11

Pam leaned over and told me I looked like a slut in my crop top
leaning against Mitch at the party. It pissed me off but she had a
point. I should be more ladylike. I should feel better about myself.
I should not let Pam get to me.

May 20

Mitch and I had a very serious talk where he said how "hard it is" and a "burden" because I won't have sex with him. Well, I told him he was free to carry his burden to someone else—Bonnie Dell, for instance.

May 21

Tommy went to the senior prom with Betsy. He wore a tux. His legs looked about a million miles long.

May 22

For Mitch, a disagreement isn't over until it's *over*. He believes an argument is fought from two sides, until someone wins & someone loses.

May 24

Mitch actually broke up with me. He thinks this is going to change my mind about having sex with him.

June 1

Mitch wants to get back together. I told him I thought we should both give it some time.

June 2

In my nightmare, I realize that Rex is still in the pen over the levee, and he's been there all this time and he's been slowly starving to death and it's my fault. I wake up feeling guilty, like I'm going to hell.

June 6

Mama told me that in her Sunday School class they talked about race relations. All the ladies were saying, "You know we all love black people." And Mama said she had the *best* idea. Her idea was for her Sunday School class to work up an exchange with a black

Sunday School class and they could go there and the black ladies could come to our church and they could have lessons and discussions and could get to know each other on a personal basis. She said she told her idea to the class and the other ladies looked at her and then went on like it had never been said. Even Miss Maydell who runs the class didn't say anything.

June 8
Daddy got a CB radio and his handle is "Mac the Knife." Daddy has an unusual sense of humor.

June 9
If you laugh at something Sara does, she does it again and again, and it's very *funny* until it's *very* annoying.

June 20
Coach Richards is marrying Karen Berger (varsity cheerleader) and she is pregnant. Big mistake.

July 1
The Regals down the street have only one key to their house and for fifteen years they have kept it in a potted plant by the back door. Last week, they were out of town and the plant finally died and their yardman threw it out. When they got home, there was no plant and no key, and they had to break into their own house.

July 3
Conversation with Tommy:

T: "I've tried to fall in love with you."
M: "You have?"
T: "Yeah, that would be nice I think."

M: "It would be."

T: "I've had dreams about you."

M: "Really?"

T: "But they're not about sex."

M: "Too bad for you."

T: "Do you think we should have an affair?"

M: "No . . . I don't think it would work out."

T: "Neither do I."

M: "It would solve a lot of problems though."

T: "No kidding."

July 5

I'm sitting on the ridge at the back of the horse pen & it's hot & humid and smells like horse shit. I love this place.

July 7

I got a new pair of Levi's and I've washed them three times, but it still feels like I'm wearing cardboard.

July 9

Stella brought home a boyfriend named Jim and we all like him. He can make her laugh at herself, and even though he's Jewish, I'm pretty sure that qualifies as a miracle.

July 10

Big fight at the house today! Jim and Stella want to travel in the west together & Mother and Daddy think it's wrong to do that if you're not married. I think Stella finally realized how much it would hurt Mama & Daddy and she's not going to do it.

July 11

Stella and Jim and I were watching TV tonight & there was this old movie on about Glenn Miller. In the movie, Jimmy Stewart

(Glenn Miller) kept saying to his wife that he was looking for this "sound" but he didn't know what it was yet. Then there was a scene where he is forced to hire more horns for a gig because he loses some of his string section, and when the band plays (with the extra horns) he hears the "sound" and he *knows* it's the "sound" and he's so happy. *I got so excited!* I said to Stella and Jim, "Have you ever felt like that?" And they both looked at me and said, "No."

July 13
Bill has a girlfriend. This seems to be improving his personal hygiene.

July 14
Stella is moving to Kansas to be near Jim. Moving to Kansas seems funny to me, I guess because of Dorothy and Toto.

August 7
I haven't written in a while. It's been a strange summer. Mitch and I are back together. The Bengal Belles went to drill team camp and I was selected as "Most Outstanding Dancer" in my category and got a big trophy that's up to my waist. Now I'm in the *Who's Who of American Drill Teams.*

August 12
I am seventeen today. Daddy took us to the Pagoda to eat and Mitch was invited. Daddy is not the easiest person to get along with, but he likes Mitch. Daddy took Mitch with him to make rounds at the hospital last Saturday and then they played golf together. It's irritating that the only person Mitch fights with is me.

August 14
Mitch told me he feels my love for God separates us because it's so deep.

August 15
Mitch & I have decided not to fight anymore.

August 20
I feel tied down with Mitch.

August 22
I'm uncomfortable with my life.

August 23
Sometimes I feel like I'm just another competition that Mitch is trying to win.

August 24
> I made a promise, I think it was last night
> Between my headache and the twisted sheets,
> I aimed for flight—and begged for peace.

August 25
Ring-around-the-rosy, I fall down. Tommy is leaving and I'm a selfish girl.

August 29
Tommy is more than a friend—he's my reflection.

August 30
I have this frightening feeling that when Tommy leaves, some part of my life is ending forever.

August 31

There are two people, a man & woman, naked on a beach. (I am not one of them.) They lie down to sleep, but they are attacked by ants. The couple runs for the ocean. The man dives in & escapes, but the woman is captured, and I think she dies. That was my dream.

September 1

When I was saying good-bye, I handed Tommy a note that said that I would come closer to dying for him than for anyone else in the world. He hugged me and said that I didn't have to die just because he was going to college.

September 2

Now I lay me down to sleep I hope.

September 3

I miss Tommy. I remember how it felt when he went to first grade a year before me. I was still in kindergarten, which was only for half a day, and I would sit at the end of the driveway at 3 o'clock and wait for the school bus to bring him home so we could play. (I want Tommy to come home to play.)

September 4

Angela said to me today that maybe we're too close. God, *please* don't let me lose Angela.

September 5

      (Poem for Angela)
      Maybe we have told too many secrets—
      My misadventures, your pained efforts,
      Our mutual need for comfort.

Perhaps, our small love we have held too tightly,
Packed too densely and unwisely
Tried to cushion the tender growing
We should have done,
At least a little on our own?

September 6

I went to the Home Economics classroom today to find Angela
(I've never been in there) and there is a bulletin board at the front
of the room that says: "MARRIAGE Is The Center Of Your LIFE!"
The word "center" is in a circle that is actually a big wedding ring
with a diamond on it. The wedding ring has strings connecting it
to pictures cut out of magazines. There are pictures of a man, children, a house, a dove holding an olive branch, a heart, and a smi-
ley face.

September 7

Mama says she doesn't wear her wedding ring because it gives her
a rash.

September 10

Met with the guidance counselor Miss Douchette (aka Miss
Douche Bag) and she gave me no guidance whatsoever.

September 16

Mitch got a jeep convertible, and he's calling himself Mario Mitch
Andretti. We're fighting big time.

September 18

I'm interested in Trinity University in San Antonio. Mainly because I don't know anyone else who's going there. I'm going to apply for early admission and get it over with.

November 1

Bill is fifteen today. I was with Daddy almost six hours last Saturday and only saw him sit down once, which was for lunch.

November 2

Jimmy Carter was elected president and Daddy said he won because it was such a beautiful day all over the South. This would seem to suggest a connection between the presidency of the United States and the frizziness of my hair.

November 4

I'm flying to San Antonio to visit Trinity in a couple of days and I can't *wait* to be somewhere on my own.

November 5

My first plane trip was like being on a roller coaster that went up and didn't come down for two hours.

November 7

The first day on a campus tour, I met a boy named Abraham (as in Lincoln). He was with a group of students that included his girlfriend, and while we were talking to them, he *winked* at me. Today, I was stretching after a jog on the track, and Abraham walked over and stood next to me. Then he took off his shirt! He had a *very* nice, very muscular body and his army pants hung down below the top of his boxers. He smiled and he had crooked teeth. His eyes were almost black. He stood very close to me, which I found threatening, but also sort of sexy.

A: "Helloooo there." (exaggerated pick-up tone of voice)
M: "Hey."

A: "You run?"

M: "Do you?"

A: "Yeah . . . Mostly after buses."

M: (laugh)

A: "I've decided to call you Slim."

M: "Are we that friendly?"

A: "We could be."

M: "I liked your girlfriend, Abraham."

A: "I like her too. I'll probably marry her. Want to go camping this weekend, Slim?"

M: "Gee, I'd love to . . . but I'm in high school."

A: "Did I mention that I'm Phi Beta Kappa?"

M: "You did."

A: "And that I can bench press a hundred pounds over my body weight?"

M: "That's very interesting."

A: "I want to make sure I make an impression."

M: "You have."

November 25

I forgot to write that I was elected Homecoming Queen a couple of weeks ago.—Senior year is a strange time of life.

November 26

The Shriners called and wanted to sponsor me in a beauty pageant, but Daddy said "No." Bill said, "Shouldn't she at least think about it?" Daddy said, "No."

November 27

I don't think I look like who I really am. But Bonnie Dell seems to prove the point that sometimes what you see is what you get.

November 28
We got the official Homecoming pictures back and there's one photo of me walking down the aisle at assembly (smiling like a Barbie doll) and the kids on either side of the aisle are clapping, but none of the girls is smiling. It's upsetting to me.

November 29
I don't want to bother anyone with how I feel. I see no use in it. But I'm thinking I may be losing control of my mind.

November 30
Mitch wanted to give me an engagement ring for Christmas but I said no, so then he said he'd give me a promise ring but I said no.

December 1
A lot of the time with Mitch, I'm a real ass.

December 2
Today we celebrated Sara's birthday and Ellen T. told the story of how Mama found out she was pregnant. Mama thought she had a virus, but it went on and on and on and so she started to wonder. She asked Ellen to take a urine sample to the doctor, and when Ellen came back from the doctor, she walked into Mama's bedroom with a bouquet of flowers. When Mama saw the flowers, she burst out crying because she knew that meant she was pregnant.

December 3
Went to church with my parents. I haven't been to the Methodist church in a while, but it struck me as very muted. The pews are covered in green-gray velvet. The people were pasty-faced and the

choir was too serious. The deacons looked smug. The good side is that no one noticed me.

December 6
Finished *Bury My Heart at Wounded Knee.* I think it changed my life, but it didn't exactly improve my mood.

December 10
A new hair salon opened right next to Safeway and it's called Do or Dye. I love that.

December 11
We took Sara to the Boat and Toy Shop today and it's just like I remembered it. The fishing boats were outside, the toys were inside, and the blind squirrel was still running around the wheel in his cage.

December 14
We got a Christmas card from the widow across the street and she signed it, "Mrs. *Paul* Fusco." She moved here by herself four years ago and no one in the neighborhood knows her real first name. I think that's funny, but then I often feel like I'm laughing at jokes that no one else hears.

December 16
I've been accepted to Trinity as a *President's Scholar*!! I'll wait and tell Mitch tomorrow. I feel sooooooo GREAT!

December 17
Mitch is in agony. I feel cruel.

December 18
The family was happy tonight.

December 19
Tommy is home for Christmas break. He *loves* college and he has new friends. Some of them are actors. It's SO good to see him!

December 20
A teenager tried to swim across the Ouachita River and almost drowned. Drowning would be an awful way to die, way too slow.

December 21
Jackson is home for Christmas break and he called and asked me to get something to eat with him tonight. This surprised me because we haven't talked or written much in the last year, not since I started dating Mitch. Anyway, we ate at the Vagabond. I told him straight out that I thought things in my life were going to work out. He asked why I thought that. When I told him I didn't have a *logical* argument for it, he said, "No, Margaret, tell me *why* do you feel your life will work out? Give me *reasons*." I sat there for several minutes and then said, "You don't really expect me to answer that, do you?" But he did. And I started to feel angry so I said we should leave, and we did, and in the car Jackson was rambling away about God's intentions. I couldn't bring myself to say anything. I can't help it if I don't know where my life is taking me.

December 24
In church tonight, I cried off & on during the whole midnight service. (People must have thought I was crazy or someone died.) I want to do better with my life.

December 25
Mitch gave me a portable TV for Christmas. (go figure)

December 27

It doesn't take a Ouija board to see that Jackson and Yvonne are becoming a couple. Maybe *that's* why he wanted to talk to me?

December 29

Just because my specially made quilt (Jackson) got ripped off in the night, I don't think I should cling to my electric blanket (Mitch). But the real question is why am I so cold?

December 31

It's after midnight. Mitch sent me a dozen red roses today and we had dinner here with Angela and her boyfriend Eric. I felt in love tonight. I felt in love with both Mitch and Angela. But there are bad things in my heart that I need to get rid of.

1977

"It all comes down to you."

January 1

Angela and I are close but I want us to be closer. I'm caught inside
to the point where I'll be talking to her and my body will shake like
some sort of body spasm. When did all of this start? It seems very
long ago, but I think it's only been recently. It's just that I don't
recall having these feelings until the moment I knew I always had.

January 2

Jackson came by today. We sat in my room and he told me about a
night over two years ago when there was a prayer meeting by the
bayou. He said that at the time he was "very fiery and prophet-
like" (true) and he was walking down by the water and God whispered in his ear "patience" clear as day. I was walking somewhere
by the water too, he said, and along with that word came an image
of me that he couldn't shake, even though girls were the last thing
he wanted to think about.

I remember that night.

January 3

Two and a half years ago—May 2, 1974—I wrote in my diary: "We
had a prayer meeting down by the bayou. It was very peaceful. I've
never written this before, but I think I'm going to fall in love with
Jackson Bishop—not now but later."

I'm not surprised. Tommy is worried. Mostly, he sees Yvonne
being hurt.

January 4

Jackson and I went for a walk. It was drizzly and my hair was flying
and crazy and he was loving it. *Problem:* Jackson loves me to look
wild and be tame. Mitch wants me to look tame and be wild. *Con-
clusion:* I will never be good at math.

January 5

I have loved Jackson for a long time. I have tried *not* to love him for a long time. My heart is really fucked up.

January 6

Jackson left. I need him to go. I need to let him go.

January 7

I had a horrible nightmare involving a freight train.

January 8

Making rounds at the hospital with Daddy, we don't talk. Daddy leads and I follow. We walk into room 520. I stand against the wall as Daddy moves toward the bed. He pushes the corner of the mattress aside and props his foot up so he can lay the clipboard on his knee. He licks his index finger and flips through the pages. "Mrs. Davis?" he says, without looking up, but the room is empty. I hear the toilet flush, and a very thin small woman walks out of the bathroom in a nylon nightie with a matching robe. She sits on the bed, her hands clasped in front of her. Daddy writes on the pages. Mrs. Davis looks at me and touches her head. "You have pretty hair," she says quietly. "Thank you," I mouth without making a sound. Daddy looks at Mrs. Davis and explains that she must have more surgery. I look back and forth between them. She is clearly worried. Daddy furrows his forehead and uses his hands to explain further, points to the part of her arm where he will operate, says exactly what he will do. Then he is finished and says, "OK. We'll be seeing you then." He walks out into the hallway, resumes a quick pace, towards another room, already flipping through the pages of the next clipboard.

January 9

(1:32 a.m.) I've got to learn *not* to think about complicated things at night because I wind up bouncing off the walls between exhausted and wired & the house is so dark and quiet that it feels dead—so I begin to feel I might *be dead*—or dreaming, only dreaming would be *good* because it would mean I was *asleep*—sleep being good—and *anything* being better than this silent pitch of utter *loneliness*. I could get a fish tank.—Except I don't want to deal with the scum.

January 10

I ache for Tommy and Jackson and me to be together like we were. Even though it was complicated, it *was* good.

January 12

Letter from Jackson: "I've given a lot of thought to the idea of becoming a minister—sometimes I have a very *definite* feeling that God has called me to take a stand. And I often think of you being with me. I'm not begging or pleading. I no longer fear your independence. Please don't ever be afraid to pursue your own goals—but I must say, I think I need you. I hope I'm not scaring you. I'm sort of scaring me."

Too late.

January 13

Being a minister suits Jackson, and being an artist suits Tommy. Angela is going to be a dental hygienist. Mitch wants to be a doctor. Bill might be a lawyer. I think I'll be an Indian chief.

January 14

There was a funeral at Bethany Baptist for an old man (Mr. Robineaux) who had a huge family. At the church, everyone was sitting in the pews waiting when two men carried down the flower arrangements. There were daisies and carnations and a huge arrangement of red mums with a banner that read "Beloved Husband and Father." I could hear someone near the front crying, "Daddy . . . Daddy . . ." The two men set up a kind of metal table with accordion folding legs at the very front, then they left and returned with the casket. A young woman stood up and wailed, "Grandpa!" and the people sitting next to her pulled her back down. I heard her crying, "Grandpa! Don't let me see him. No . . ." The men turned to the casket, opened it, removed a white cloth over the old man's face, and adjusted his hands. His wife stood up from the front row and walked slowly over to the open casket with her son and grandson. The father motioned to another child to join them, but the boy in the pew shook his head and stared down at the ground. I didn't go up to the casket either. But I could see his dead body from where I was. It wasn't as awful as I thought it would be, but it made me think.

January 15
What point am I missing about love?

January 16
I thought about Jackson too much today.

January 17
> Our love unsynchronized is unwieldy, and we
> Left only to ourselves, do watch and wait and pace
> This pause of longing—breathe—we sink. Repeat.
> It is something like I imagine drowning must be.

January 18
At dinner, my father was talking to Bill about his grades, saying, "If you want to get into medical school, son, you need to do

better." And suddenly Bill stood up and said, "What makes you so *sure* this *ISN'T* the best I can do?" Then he walked out and no one said anything for the rest of the meal. What bothers me is that Daddy makes Bill feel retarded if he doesn't make A's, and I do make A's, and Daddy barely notices.

January 19
Everyone is tense around here.

January 20
I overheard my mother say to Aunt Lou that if she had had dogs before she'd had children, she might never have had children.

January 22
When we were little, Tommy and I believed we had magical powers. The secret sign was having a mole on your neck, which, conveniently, we both have. The secret sign meant you were a witch. Being witches, we did all kinds of things—due to our magical powers. We traveled through time and we could fly. To prove we could fly, we would run down the hallway, jump from the doorway of my room, soar above the shag carpet, and land on my bed. *That* was the true test of flight.

January 24
Watching a miniseries on TV called *Roots* about slaves and slavery. Everyone is talking about it. Some people are upset about it.

January 25
There have been rumors flying around school that some black kids might do something violent because of *Roots* and some white parents are keeping their kids home from school, which is not helping the situation.

January 28

Today in Advanced English, this girl named Sharon called Emily Dickinson "a weirdo who was crazy." How ignorant!!!! I *argued* with her, but Miss Austin didn't say much of anything. I've started to not like Miss Austin. I definitely dislike Sharon.

January 29

Mitch came over this morning and Daddy asked *him* to go make rounds. And Mitch did.

February 8

I've noticed that I have a hard time arguing without getting emotional and I argue too much. I want to train my mind to think in a more logical fashion, so I can express myself and be understood. Today in English class, I was trying to explain the emotional experience of beauty, the pain—is this the wrong word?—in beauty, and I couldn't do it. I didn't mean pain in a negative way, but as a kind of heartache. My thoughts are so haphazard and I need to learn to listen better. Plus I blurt.

February 11

Today, Wanda said, "Margaret, you never let anyone in, do you?" She didn't say it to hurt me . . . because she knew I knew what she meant. And it does frighten me . . . my ability to stay emotionally separate, even from people I care about.

February 12

I must be a burden to my friends. I always want to defend myself and explain myself. I separate myself from other people's lives. Why do I do that? It amazes me what I don't feel.

February 18
Bonnie Dell has been spreading a rumor about me. The rumor doesn't bother me. It's knowing how much she wants to hurt me that actually hurts. Maybe I need to get my priorities straight?

February 20
Mitch said he knew he was lacking something so he came with me to Bethany Baptist. He got baptized in the Holy Spirit. This is a good thing.

February 21
I have off-campus privileges until graduation and all month I've been coming home for lunch and watching *The Young and the Restless.* Mama *hates* it, but it's the highlight of my day.

February 24
Angela and I are close—but I want us to be closer.

February 26
Mama, Sara, and I visited Uncle Fred and Aunt Emmeline in their tiny house in West Monroe. Uncle Fred is very fit looking for an elderly man, and today he was dressed in a striped golf shirt, brown polyester pants, & pale blue socks. Aunt Em wears leisure suits and Coke-bottle-thick glasses and her fingers are bent sideways with arthritis, but she giggles like a girl. We got there around 10:30 in the morning, and Aunt Em gave me a Coke. Uncle Fred offered Mama coffee, then iced tea, and then whiskey.

February 27
I have this overwhelming desire to *do* things. Some people think of this as a problem.

March 1

Aunt Beth killed herself—sixteen years ago! And I just found out today! I thought she died of cancer . . . or something. When I asked Mama *why* no one told me before, she said, "It's not that it was hidden, Margaret. It just never came up."

March 2

I asked Mama if there were *other* things about my family that I might want to know before I die or get married?? She was *perturbed*. She said, "Well, your great-aunt Snookie, the fat one in the pictures? She used to be *skinny* . . . she only got fat after the lobotomy."

March 3

The dictionary defines *psychosis* (which is, or *was*, according to my father, a medical reason for performing a lobotomy) as "a major mental disorder in which the personality is very seriously disorganized and contact with reality is usually impaired." (I do not find this comforting.)

March 4

On Fridays some kids gather behind the band room at lunchtime to smoke cigarettes and some get stoned. Today, I went over to talk to Tony and he offered me a joint. I thought it over for half a second but refused. Then he said, "I've always wanted to sleep with you." I wasn't exactly sure what he meant, so I asked, "In what way?" He said, "I thought there was only one way."

March 6

Tony waited by the track this afternoon for me to finish jogging. Then he bawled me out. He told me that I'm *too friendly* and boys misread it. He said he was setting me straight for my own good. I listened and tried not to be defensive. It was good advice, I guess.

March 8
I may be counting too much on the fact that college will be different from high school.

March 9
Bonnie Dell has made me realize something this year. There are lots of people (millions and millions) that don't want to be my friend. Each person is like a planet around which things revolve that the person chooses. Actually, that would be the sun . . . so . . . OK, if you are like a *planet*, then you are your own world, with different people living on different continents, connected to you, but not necessarily to each another. *But* any one of those people could set off a nuclear bomb, and the fallout from one bomb *could* potentially so damage the planet that it could become uninhabitable. Then the planet would die.

March 10
Miss Austin gave me an A / D– on my Hamlet paper! She said it was a good paper (A), but not the one she assigned (D–) . . . I try to convince myself that losing every now and then makes you a better person, but I don't believe me.

March 11
There is an old love letter in Great-Grandma Beulah's trunk, a letter to Aunt Snookie from someone named George. And what I wonder is did he write the letter before or after she got fat?

> October 17, 1925
> Dear Snookie,
> Here begins a supplication for peace. I approach with due humility that which is doubtlessly a hostile camp. What

must you have thought of my prolonged silence? I am, perhaps, now confronted with your contempt, and so I ask your forgiveness.

After considerable trotting around, I received your letter and enjoyed it very much. Now, after considerably more trotting around and back again, I am answering it—I was stumped at the cold logic you employed to refute my erstwhile statements concerning your beauty and loveliness as a woman. The trend of my letters apparently does not flow in convincing channels.

Tout à vous,
George

March 12
In my mind, I try to understand love, but in my heart, I'm confounded. I would feel a certain lack in my life without Mitch, but I don't know if that means I love him.

March 13
Why is logic always considered cold?

March 14
> Desire unspent—
> It feels like years and years of it.

March 15
Watching Daddy hit his plastic golf balls in the backyard today. (I was fetching.) I asked him, "How do you know when you're in love?" Daddy stopped, leaned on his golf club, and said that for him it was like in that movie where they say: "Love means never having to say you're sorry." Then he hit the rest of his balls.

March 16

Mama was in the laundry room ironing and I told her what Daddy said yesterday. At first she got quiet, then she said, "That line never did make any sense to me."

March 17

I asked Mama if she thought I should marry Mitch, and she said that if I was ready to marry him, I wouldn't be asking. She said, "Even you must realize that he has to work hard to keep you interested."

March 19

Have been avoiding Mitch.

March 20

There was a surprise for me tonight. Angela walked in the house after dinner and she screamed, "I'm in love!" Then she explained the way that her relationship with Eric is so perfect. I'm trying to be happy for her, but right now there's a distance between us, and a sense of misunderstanding. Our roads seem very opposite.

March 21

On the way to school this morning, Angela told me that her ankle hurt. Then, when she found a great parking space right next to school, she said she *knew* God had provided it for her so she wouldn't have to walk so far. Stuff like this is starting to get on my nerves. It's not that I think Angela was wrong, it's just lately I'm so critical of everybody. I'm hoping people will just avoid me. I want to get away—be *free*. It hurts me that I'm hurting Mitch because I know he doesn't understand.

March 22

Conversation with Mother:

ME: "I don't understand the way boys think of girls as their
possessions."

MAMA: "Boys and girls are just different."

ME: "Tommy and I aren't that different."

MAMA: "You and Tommy *are* different, just not from each
other."

ME: "What's that supposed to mean?"

MAMA: "I don't know, Margaret."

ME: "Are you trying to confuse me on purpose?"

MAMA: "No, if I'm confusing you, it's entirely by accident. All
I'm saying is that life isn't always easy to figure out."

ME: "Well, that's *comforting*."

March 25

Wanda and I talked today about something that's been *bothering*
me. I wanted to know if Doug Reed really did stick his hands down
her pants (two years ago?). I asked her and she said it was at the
church one night and she was standing at the water fountain and
had on her striped overalls with her red-and-white cowboy shirt
that she'd cut off short, and he came up behind her and put his
hands down on either side of her pants and crossed his hands in
front. (feeling a little sick)

March 30

Today was the Bengal Belles' last performance. It sort of broke my
heart.

March 31

This morning Mama was ragging on me about my room and I tried
to make a joke and said, "Is there a *reason* you're in such a good
mood, Mama, or are you just being nice for my sake?" And she
grounded me.

April 1
Stella is unhappy at her job. (The sigh of Jonah.)

April 3
The thing that hurts is that Mama & Daddy don't know how to take care of Bill. Bill tries hard. It only looks like carelessness.

April 4
Walked in on Mama crying and cussing to herself in the kitchen. We ended up talking. I never knew that Mama felt guilty about Aunt Lou, and also about Stella. Mama said she was overwhelmed by having babies so young, and that bore down particularly on Stella. She apologized for telling me these things, but it didn't upset me.

April 6
Sara is an extremely loud child and talks nonstop. This results in my taking lots of walks. The good thing is that walking makes me feel better. And trees never talk.

April 7
Even Jesus had to go into the wilderness before he could find himself. I think someday I will *have* to let myself go. It's the getting myself back that I'm worried about.

April 10
I'm a weak person. That's why there's hostility in me.

April 12
Of all the boys in my life, Tommy is the most relevant. Jackson is who my heart wants to love. I care deeply for Mitch, but how deep is enough?

April 13
The pastor at Bethany Baptist tried to preach us all into *Hell* tonight in less than an hour, but for *some* reason his words just did not flow in *convincing channels.*

April 17
I looked in at Mama's Sunday School class this morning. All the ladies were wearing bright colored dresses and had red lips . . . and when they turned and smiled at me in the doorway, I felt like I was looking at a bunch of Easter eggs.

April 18
"SERVICE IS NOT SPELLED SERVE US" (marquee in front of Riverside Baptist).

April 24
What I learned in church today: Grown women should not be allowed to wear bows in their hair.

April 26
I'm praying for Angela & Tommy & my family & for our government officials & former President Nixon & the boy whose arm was sewn back on.

April 28
Conversation with Mama:

MAMA: "Jo Ann Matthews said her son saw you at church Sunday & wanted to marry you."
ME: "He doesn't even know me. Why would he say that?"
MAMA: "I think it's the way you look, Margaret, you're so pretty and frail. You look so vulnerable, and that makes people

want to take care of you. I think it's why boys are so attracted to you."

ME: "Boys are not so attracted to me."

MAMA: (shrug)

ME: "And I'm not *so* vulnerable."

MAMA: "I'm just saying it's what people see."

ME: "Maybe people *see* what they *want* to see."

MAMA: "People usually do."

May 5

Done with high school.

May 6

At dinner, Daddy said, "I'm confident life will never be dull for you." Then he gave me a calculator.

May 7

Angela thinks sororities are a good way to make friends. I think sororities are fine, but I want to find my own friends.

May 8

Hand-painted sign at a fish stand on LaSalle Street:

GAR GOO CATFISH BUFFALO

May 9

I went by the Junior Shop to talk to Mrs. Lipton about working over the summer, and in the back, Sharon, the full-time salesgirl, told me that she had an abortion a few weeks ago. She said her boyfriend wouldn't help, so Mrs. Lipton lent her the money and she went to Dallas to do it.

May 11

Aunt Lou is feeling bad again.

May 12

Momma Doll finally finished my prom dress. (I was worried she wouldn't.) I *love* it. It's a gypsy dress—like my favorite Halloween costume grown up, like it was made from scarves sewn together. When I put it on and hugged her, she said, "Now you have yourself a *big* time!"

May 15

Talked to Tommy on the phone tonight. (He's in finals and gets home next week.) He's so excited about me going to Trinity next year. He says I'll love college. BUT he says when I get there, I need to tone down my *accent*. (I didn't know I had an accent.) He told me the story of his family on their ski trip last winter and Ellen lining all the kids up in the airport and making them repeat, "I'm from mon-ROE, lou-EASY-anna." Ellen told them all that if they said it the *normal* way—MON-roe, LOU-zeeanna—then people would think they were hicks.

May 16

Why is it we work so hard to be interesting to one another?

May 17

Aunt Lou is coming to graduation, so I think she's doing OK. Angela and I will sit next to each other on stage. (The top ten percent of the class sits on stage.)

May 18

I'm giving the invocation at the graduation ceremony. I'm sure they asked me because I'm the only kid willing to pray out loud who doesn't hand out pamphlets on the Second Coming.

May 20

The prom was fine and fun and everything. Mitch rented a room at the Howard Johnson & after the dance we went there & drank too much & things happened. Various, *non-pregnantizing* (I think I made that word up) sex things happened. It wasn't just him and I don't feel bad or good about it, but it's not what I want in my life right now and I don't think what happened should happen again. That's what I've decided.

May 22

It's the sex thing. Mitch is really pressuring me & I wish he would stop because it only confuses me.

May 23

I've found a way to help me fall asleep at night. I say the Lord's Prayer over and over.

May 24

Sign outside a building near downtown Monroe:
BECOME A MORTGAGE LOAN OFFICER CALL 322-3476 JESUS SAVES

May 25

When I look at myself in the mirror in my bathroom, I get the sense my mind (me) is looking out of a window (my eyes) and it makes me wonder if I might be living my life in someone else's body?

May 27

It's all fighting with Mitch now, but when I suggest splitting up, the fighting only gets worse.

May 28
Tommy is home and Jackson is too and they are always together so I keep running into Jackson. It's strange with him . . . because there's still something there.

May 29
I asked Mother if she & Daddy fought when they were first married. She said it's hard to describe their disagreements as fights because they never talked about them. She told me about once, when they had three kids, and no dishwasher, and her hands were getting a rash, so she told Daddy he *had* to wash the dishes for her & he did do them for a few nights. Until one night when she was putting one of us to sleep, she heard a crash, and it was Daddy, who had gotten so mad he broke a dish against the counter. He never said anything about it and he never did the dishes again.

May 30
I'm working at the Junior Shop for the summer. Tommy has a job at the hospital. Mitch is working at Popeyes Chicken. Bill is digging swimming pools.

May 31
I told Tommy I would be lying if I pretended not to have strong feelings for Jackson, and Tommy said maybe I should lie.

June 1
Alone seems to be a theme in my thoughts. I wonder: Can you be alone when you are physically with someone? I think you can because *alone* is a state of being based in the idea that something is missing. Or it can also be a state of mind based in the feeling that you are missing something. So feeling alone has nothing to do

with whether or not you are in the presence of someone, unless the someone you miss is the someone who is not in your presence.

June 2
". . . my soul thirsts for thee, my flesh longs for thee in a dry and thirsty land . . ." (Psalms 63:1)

I miss *him*.

June 4
Mitch works at night from 5 to 10:30 p.m. so we hardly see one another. The good (or not so good) part is that I wind up seeing Jackson, because he's at Tommy's house. I ask myself—If I feel this much for Jackson, why am I so involved with Mitch?

June 5
Jackson and I went to breakfast this morning at 6 a.m. We ended up driving out in the country down dirt roads and talking for hours. I'm truly afraid that these feelings for Jackson will bring out the worst side of me—maybe of all of us.

June 6
Tommy had lunch with Jackson at the Piccadilly and he said Jackson spent most of his questions asking about me. Tommy thinks Jackson is still in love with me, or he's in love with what I "represent to him." Since I had no earthly idea what Tommy was talking about, he explained it. He said, "You're a free spirit, Maggie, and now Jackson is going to be a minister, and he'll likely wind up in a church full of old people. Think about it."

I don't feel *the least bit* free.

June 7
These great waves of depression settle on me & I'm critical of everything. I only weigh 107 pounds, but I feel heavy.

June 8

I asked Mama if I should talk to a doctor about my feeling depressed and she said she thought I just needed to get more sleep.

June 9

I asked Daddy if I could see a psychiatrist because I'm sort of worried about this bad feeling I have about myself. He said, "No." He was in bed watching TV and he kept right on watching. He couldn't even look at me. Sometimes I think I hate my father as much as I love him.

June 10

Daddy came into my room and sat on my bed and talked to me. He told me that it's normal for kids my age to have self-doubts & that there is a big gap between being sick and being insecure. He told me he was willing to let me see a psychiatrist, but in his experience most psychiatrists are more in need of treatment than their patients.

June 11

Went over to Tommy's house when I got off work and Jackson and Yvonne were there. It was bad. I felt like a small child. When I told a story and Tommy acted uninterested, it *killed* me. Later, Tommy said he was just tired and I took it the wrong way. I told him reality counts for very little in the face of psychosis.

June 12

Mitch and I are cooling things. It's good some and bad some. I'm in no frame of mind to be involved with *anyone.*

June 13

As I write this, the sun is coming up. I went over to Tommy's after dinner last night and Jackson was there and we played gin rummy until around midnight. Then Tommy went to bed and Jackson and I stayed up all night talking.

June 14

Note from Tommy I found in an envelope on my pillow today:

> This is a common, ordinary note. It has nothing to set
> it apart from the thousands of notes you will receive
> during your lifetime. Yet, in its own mysterious way, it
> compels you to read on. You must find out what it is about.
> I suggest you meet me on the tennis court at 9 p.m. and
> wear your dancing shoes. Will you come? Take your time
> to decide. The fact that I know all your secrets and have
> access to a public address system shouldn't enter into the
> matter.—The Boy Next Door

Thank God for Tommy.

June 15

Tony came by tonight and we decided to go drinking and driving
around and wound up parked in the park. We were talking and I
kissed him. I could tell Tony was confused about whether or not to
kiss me back, but I knew exactly what I was doing. A kiss is not a
commitment though. It didn't mean anything.

June 16

In the grocery store someone asked Mother if Sara was her grand-
baby. Mama said, "No, she's *my* baby." The lady said, "Oh, it *always* feels like that." Mama nodded and didn't argue and I'm sure
the lady thought Sara was *my* baby.—*My life is steamrolling me.*

June 17

It's easy to see that my depression comes in cycles. I'll be high
for a few days & then WHAM! I fall apart. What I need to do is
apply discipline so that when I no longer feel happy, I can

convince myself that there is some reason to be happy & act accordingly.

June 18

I'll admit it. I need to feel attractive. It's a selfish desire, but it's true. (I'm a little worried about these conversations I'm having with myself.)

June 19

SHIT! What do I do? Ellen just stopped me in the driveway and started asking me about Tommy. The usual, like how did I think he was doing at college. Has he mentioned to me if he's dating anyone? . . . Then she asked me right out if Tommy was *homosexual*. Without even thinking, I said, "No!"

"Why would you think that, Ellen?"

"Well, Tommy has always been different, Margaret."

"Since when?"

"Since he was small, four or five."

"Four or five years old?!"

"Yes, and there's his relationship with you, for instance."

"His relationship with *me*?"

"Margaret, it's fine. I've always thought Tommy was homosexual . . . and it's no big deal really."

"But I still don't understand *why* you think that."

"It just seems that he *is*, Margaret."

This is weird. But I'm going to try not to worry about it.

June 20

I'm worrying. I keep thinking about all those homosexual boys in Texas who were murdered and buried in the sand. I'm going to smoke a cigarette.

June 21

PEOPLE WHO ARE MOST IMPORTANT TO ME:

1. Mama
2. Daddy
3. Tommy
4. ~~Jackson~~ Angela
5. Sara
6. ~~Angela~~ Jackson
7. ~~Mitch~~ Bill
8. Stella
9. Mary
10. Mitch

PEOPLE WHO ARE LEAST IMPORTANT TO ME:

1. Bonnie Dell
2. Ted (this guy who follows me around and is perverted)
3. Steve (my cousin's jerk boyfriend who got her pregnant)
4. Oral Roberts

June 22

While cleaning up the kitchen after dinner:

ME: "The other day Ellen asked me if Tommy was homosexual."
MAMA: "Is he?"
ME: "You're not *surprised* she asked?"
MAMA: "I don't think anyone would be too surprised."
ME: "Well, *I* was surprised . . . I don't think he's homosexual."
MAMA: "That's fine."
ME: "But *you* think he is, don't you?"
MAMA: "I think you should talk to Tommy."
ME: "Mama . . . there's no way I can do that."

MAMA: "I'm sure there is."

ME: "You know, this is *not* helping!"

MAMA: "Talk to Tommy, Margaret, before you panic."

ME: "You think I'm *panicking?*"

MAMA: "Yes, I do . . . a little."

June 23

Tried to kill myself today. Rode my bike twenty miles to Moon Lake and back at 4 o'clock in the afternoon & almost had a heat stroke. Barely made it home.

June 24

Tonight I tried to talk to Mitch about how he is better off without me, but he was so hurt the conversation didn't go anywhere. My life isn't going too well.

June 25

This afternoon the wind started blowing the leaves in the trees and a dark cloud moved in, covering the entire sky. The colors outside are all muted now . . . but the air is bright so everything seems clearer, more in focus. I *want* to talk to Tommy, but I don't see how.

June 26

Tommy & I went for a walk on the levee and I told him I thought I might be homosexual. I don't know why I said it exactly, but I do think it might be true. A bunch of things make me wonder. Tommy said, "Margaret, I think that you are *not* homosexual. You're straight." I said, "Does it matter?" He said, "Well . . . if *I'm* not straight, does it matter to *you?*" Without thinking, I said, "*No* . . . I don't care if you're straight, crooked, or a little teacup." Then we had a very long talk, and I'm too tired to write it all down, but Tommy's known for years, and he did try to tell me, but he never knew where to start. The moon was almost full tonight, but not quite.

June 27

I asked one of the pastors at Bethany Baptist what he thought about homosexuality and Christianity and he said a gay Christian is like a Jewish Nazi. That was a blow.

June 28

There is a dark dissatisfaction lurking in the back of my mind. What if I get to college and I'm not smart or good at anything?

June 29

I saw Dr. Cary, who is a psychiatrist. Mama dropped me off. I was so nervous that I spilled Coca-Cola on my shirt in the waiting room. I went to the bathroom at least four times because I was afraid I would need to pee in the middle of the session. Dr. Cary got me from the waiting room and we went to his office, which is fairly small, with a desk and two gold Naugahyde chairs (they were *ugly*) in front of the desk facing each other. We sat in the chairs. He didn't say a word for a long time and kept glancing out the window directly behind my head at the birds on his bird feeder. I think he was bored.

ME: Am I supposed to say something? I don't know what to say.
DR.: Oh?
ME: I don't know if I have anything to say.
DR.: Oh?
ME: I mean I'm not sure.
DR.: Perhaps you *don't* have anything to say?
ME: Well, I think I need help.

DR.: You came here because you thought I would help you?

ME: Yes, sir.

DR.: *Why* are you here, Margaret?

ME: Because I want someone to help me work through all this.

DR.: Work through what?

ME: Whatever is wrong with me.

DR.: What do you think is wrong with you?

ME: I don't know. I don't understand myself.

DR.: What don't you understand about yourself?

ME: I guess I don't understand my feelings.

DR.: Feeling and understanding are two different things.

ME: Right.

DR.: Maybe what you want is to *avoid* your feelings by trying to understand them?

ME: Do you think that's it?

DR.: Do *you* think that's it?

ME: It could be it.

DR.: (silence)

ME: Maybe that's why I can't cry.

DR.: You can't cry?

ME: Well, it's more that I *don't* cry. I don't want to feel what you have to feel that makes you cry.

DR.: Then what do you feel?

ME: I can't tell.

DR.: (silence)

ME: I guess it's like my brain takes over and I think to myself that being emotional won't solve whatever it is, so I try not to get emotional.

DR.: So you can control what's happening inside you?

ME: Sort of.

DR.: Oh?

ME: (pause) I can't think of what to say.

DR.: Why do you have to think first?

ME: Because I want to be clear.

DR.: Why?

(silence)

DR.: You look upset. What's wrong?

ME: I don't know.

(silence)

ME: I'm actually feeling *more* crazy right now—like I'm starting to lose it.

DR.: *Lose* it? What does that mean?

ME: It means *losing* . . . I feel like I'm *failing.* And I *hate* to fail.

DR.: How are you failing?

ME: (long pause) . . . I've lost my train of thought.

DR.: That's a clever way of avoiding the question.

ME: I'm not sure I like being here.

DR.: Why did you come here?

ME: So I could feel better.

DR.: You want me to help you feel better?

ME: Yes! That's the whole point of it. Because I feel so bad sometimes I can't stand it—and that scares me.

DR.: I can see how.

June 30

Jesus said to his disciples, "He that finds his life shall lose it, and he that loses his life for my sake shall find it." I think Jesus meant that you must lose your pride in yourself, that you should live *without* pride and *with* love. I think that's it. That's the floor plan of heaven—the map to the universe.

July 1

My whole heart aches. (weigh 105 lbs.)

July 2

After several talks, Jackson and I have agreed to try to be together. I'm not at all sure it's the right thing. I told Mitch and I've never seen him so crushed. Jackson will tell Yvonne. This will hurt people. Right now, I feel like I'm in the middle of a pain in the ass.

July 3

There was one perfect moment. Jackson and I were lying down on the levee looking up at the stars. We rolled across the grass and we kissed, and we were freer with each other than we've ever been. I said out loud, "I love you."

> (for J. B.)
> You are like fireflies
> swarming. I am
> your heart, who leaps
> wildly. I think
> (or is it your eyes?)
> that I have never been
> this happy.

July 4

Jackson and I do not exactly see eye to eye on everything, but I'm not sure how much this matters. Aunt Lou was better today. I did notice she had a couple of highballs.

July 5

After work today, I went to the library. (Sitting in a comfy chair in the library in the summer with the AC on is like sitting in a cloud.) I spent the whole time looking up definitions of religion. Some are:

1. A childhood neurosis, a form of illusion. (Sigmund Freud)
2. The opium of the people. (Karl Marx)
3. A relation to God. (Thomas Aquinas)
4. Morality touched by emotions. (Matthew Arnold)
5. What an individual does with his solitariness. (Alfred North Whitehead)

July 6

Religion is primarily a relation to God, so I believe it can, and maybe should be, solitary. Jackson believes that fellowship is crucial because Jesus said to gather in His name. I believe that sitting in a pew with people you don't know isn't particularly meaningful when you get down to it.

July 7

Saw Dr. Coldfish yesterday, and this time I tried. I think he thinks I'm spoiled.

ME: So I'm going to talk and open up.
DR.: (silence)
ME: I was thinking about what I don't like about myself and how I wish I were a stronger person, a more independent person.
DR.: (silence)
ME: Isn't that important?
DR.: Do you think it's important?
ME: I wouldn't have talked about it if I didn't think it was.
DR.: No?
ME: No.
DR.: Your motive for talking about it was to do what?
ME: To give you information so you can figure me out.
DR.: Or maybe to try and control this therapy session.

ME: (pause) I don't know what you mean.

DR.: I think you're trying to figure yourself out because it's too frightening to let me or anyone else do it for you.

ME: Why would I do that?

DR.: You tell me.

ME: (pause) Because then I wouldn't be in control?

DR.: Yes.

ME: Do you think I try to control my relationships?

DR.: Do you?

ME: I don't know . . . why would I do that?

DR.: Don't analyze it, Margaret, just feel it.

ME: So my problem is I need to learn not to analyze myself because it stops me from feeling?

DR.: That answer was a clever way of avoiding how you felt about what I just said.

ME: What is it you think I'm feeling?

DR.: I don't know. You haven't let any of that show yet.

ME: Well, I can't tell the difference . . . between when I'm analyzing or being real.

DR.: Real? What does that mean?

ME: It means . . . well, I'm not *real* with most people. Or that's not completely true because *inside* I'm real. It's just that I'm *scared*. I'm scared of practically every other person in the world . . . and I dread my life because it's so exhausting to be so scared all the time. I'm afraid . . .

DR.: (silence)

ME: . . . something is wrong with me.

DR.: We have to stop now.

July 8

My relationship with Jackson is strained, but he doesn't know the half of it.

July 9

The physical side of my relationship to Jackson isn't working. He says I'm not letting down my defenses, but I *want* to let them down. This is all too painful. I wish I could just turn my head OFF.

July 10

Ran into Mitch's mother, Mrs. Hardy, and I've *got* to get this out—she really gets on my nerves! She's always saying such aggravating things. It's always about Mitch & his girlfriends or his stupid mustache, or it's a bad-taste joke about school and the fact that I'm not going to LSU. She acts like she knows everything.—Well, I feel better now that I wrote that! I thought I was going to have to start screaming at her right there in front of the grocery store!!

July 11

How is it that I get so carried away with boys I don't love, and then with Jackson, I don't feel it? Went bowling. I'm an awful bowler. I'm an awful person.

July 12

Suicide is easy to imagine. The first time I thought about killing myself, I was around ten years old. Usually, I imagine painless options, but once I did imagine killing myself with a large kitchen knife.

July 13

Went to see Dr. Cary. When I walked into his office, I was *enveloped* with weakness, something between sadness and fear. I think I bother him.

(*Looooong* silence)
ME: Hello.
DR.: Hi.

ME: You're not going to help me get started are you?

DR.: (shrug)

ME: OK. I feel sad. But I didn't feel it until I was sitting here.

DR.: Why do you think that is?

ME: Because I'm *supposed* to feel in here?

DR.: Are you supposed to *not feel* outside of here?

ME: Maybe.

DR.: When you let yourself feel sad, how does that feel?

ME: It feels bad. I feel empty . . . lonely.

DR.: What is loneliness like?

ME: Like I'm *alone*. Like I'm sitting in an office with someone who doesn't really care about me.

DR.: (silence)

ME: And I feel like I've got to be careful . . .

DR.: (silence)

ME: Or all the people I care about will be hurt or disappointed.

DR.: Disappointed?

ME: Yes. And I'm so *tired* of being afraid of letting the people I love *down*, and them maybe *leaving* me, that I hide anything that might cause that to happen.

DR.: *Who* will be let down?

ME: I don't know.

DR.: (silence)

ME: My parents?

DR.: (silence)

ME: I wish I were closer to my parents.

DR.: (silence)

ME: I feel disconnected from them.

DR.: Disconnected?

ME: Yeah. And I want to feel connected.

DR.: And the way you feel connected to them is by longing for them?

ME: I don't understand what you mean.

DR.: Don't you?

ME: No. I guess I'm not very smart.

DR.: I think you are. I think you're so smart that you built yourself a trap. You want your parents to think you're independent so they'll be proud of you. So they *do* think you're independent and they *are* proud of you. But the result is that you don't feel a connection, because the connection you've created is based on upholding an image, and for you, maintaining that image seems to preclude showing your feelings. And if you can't show your feelings, how can you have a true connection with anyone?

ME: (silence)

DR.: (*more* silence)

ME: But I *need* my parents to be proud of me.

DR.: And do you think they are?

ME: Yes. I think so.

DR.: But that doesn't make you feel better?

ME: In some ways it does.

DR.: But you still want to feel connected?

ME: I want to, but I don't know how it works . . . *being connected.* I don't know what to believe. I don't know if I believe *you.* I don't know if it's even *worth* it, living like this. And *that* scares me.

DR.: I can see why.

July 14

Mama says that she's always been moody and that she and Stella are very similar in that way. She says Mary is the one who has always been like a ray of sunshine. She says I have always been a strong person and asked lots of questions, more like Daddy. She says I'm nothing like Aunt Lou has ever been.

July 15

Last night I dreamed I was at some kind of party. All the girls there looked glamorous and had on glamorous dresses. I was wearing a short flippy skirt made of a sheer fabric. As soon as I left the party, I realized I wasn't wearing a slip and so everyone at the party had been able to see through my skirt to my thighs and panties. When I realized this in the dream, I was surprised, but I was not embarrassed.

July 16

5 THINGS MOST IMPORTANT TO JACKSON:
Serving God
~~His Friends~~
Getting attention
Being admired
His friends
Being in the woods

5 THINGS MOST IMPORTANT TO MITCH:
Winning
His family
Having fun
Sex
~~Watching Johnny Carson~~
Sports

5 THINGS MOST IMPORTANT TO ME:
My family
My friends
My relationship to God *(this should come first)*
Being respected
~~Success~~
Being loved

July 17

I have to face it. I don't feel God in church anymore. I feel God, but mostly when I'm outside, especially in the woods or at night, or on the dark side of the levee when I can't see the ground I'm walking on.

July 18

I've decided not to go to church anymore. By doing this, I'm not sure if I'm shrinking my life or opening it up.

July 19

I look out the window in my dream & see girls. I call out the back door to them and insist they tell me what's going on. They look at each other & shrug & take me into this huge beautiful room in my own house and I think: This is *my* house, why didn't I know this was here? Next, there is a party and each girl had been assigned a boy. There are games of competition and I've been paired with Jackson, but when our eyes meet, I reveal my contempt for the whole thing in my expression, and I don't step up to be his partner. I am defiant. He steps towards me anyway and I let him, and we move together to a place out of sight and kiss passionately.

What I really remember about the dream is my *anger*.

July 20

> It's always there,
> in the whispered asides I imagine
> —the unquiet
> argument of love.

July 21

"Singers sing your heart away 'cause while sinners sin, the children play. Oh Lord how they play and play. For that happy day, for that *haaappyyy* day." (Cat Stevens)

July 22

I'm not going to see Dr. Cary anymore. Daddy says these things tend to fall into place over time. I certainly hope so.

July 23

I've got to take responsibility for the pain I've caused. I love Jackson, but I don't seem to want him, not right now anyway.

July 24

It wasn't an emotional ending. Jackson and Yvonne are back together. Personally, I *want* to be alone. (I wouldn't look twice if the Apostle Paul himself whistled at me.)

July 25

My parents aren't trying to tell me what to do and this has made things much easier between us.

July 26

Angela asked me to help her pack for LSU. When I got to her house, she had all her clothes arranged in matching outfits on the bed and hanging on the doors. . . . Matching clothes *scare* me a little. Outfits scare me *a lot.*

July 27

Last night in my dream I was caught in a flood. Tommy was in it, too. I think he was wearing a dress.

July 28

The story you are about to read is true. None of the names have been changed. No one is innocent.

> Margaret Sartor's relationship with Jackson Bishop died
> this week. The exact time of expiration is uncertain.

Symptoms first surfaced years ago and flare-ups have been common. The relationship became active again less than a month ago, and, unfortunately, it appears to have consumed itself. Both Mr. Bishop and Miss Sartor remain in critical condition. Survival is not expected. A prayer vigil will be held, but no one is invited.

July 29

It's scary to face the fact that I'm changing and becoming a person that's all my own. It's like that scene in *Mary Poppins*, just before the captain fires his cannon from the rooftop, and everyone in the house prepares for the building to tremble—and they know that when it does, it'll be a miracle if nothing breaks.

July 30

I find myself thinking about Mitch & then I don't. Mitch's family has been having some trouble lately & I got caught in the middle of it the other night. Also, I wonder about what Jackson & I could have had and what went wrong.

July 31

Part of me can't stop believing that it was my fate to be with Jackson. And if I am stepping *out* of my fate, then what or *whose* fate am I now stepping into?

August 1

I am drifting into distress.

August 2

I think I'm going to Trinity to run away from the people I love so much that my need for them is painful to me.

August 3

Jackson and I will never be lovers, yet I think I have never believed in anything more. If I was wrong about that, what other things have I been wrong about?

August 4

Tonight Momma Doll started talking about a child she needed to see about. Mama asked did she mean Sara but Momma Doll said, "You know where she is. You take me there." Later, she was fine.

August 5

I either love Jackson or I despise him, and I can't decide which is the truer emotion.

August 6

The roots of the trees by the river look just like Aunt Em's fingers bent and stuck in the mud. Having a river in your backyard is useful. You always have something to throw yourself into.

August 7

This just happened:

Rrrrrrrrrrrring
M: "Hello?"
J: "Margaret, can I come over?"
M: "It's 3 a.m., Jackson."
J: "I know. Can you meet me outside to talk?"
M: "Why?"
J: "Because I want to talk to you."

I waited, leaning against Daddy's beat-up station wagon. I actually prayed for him not to show up. Then he arrived in that catastrophic green car of his and walked over. He stood with the carport light shining on him, like he was an actor on stage.

J: "I want to tell you what I'm thinking, Margaret, how I feel."

M: "You don't have to tell me anything, Jackson. I haven't asked you to."

J: "I *want* to tell you."

M: "But it won't matter. It won't change anything."

J: "Listen, I still think about us. You made me really happy. And part of me still holds on to that."

M: "I care about you, Jackson."

J: "You care about me? Margaret . . . I feel like I'm standing in a courtroom with you. You're too distant. You make this too hard. I'm *trying* to reach out to you, and you aren't making it easy."

M: "I'm sorry about that."

Then he said it, very quietly and very fast . . . too fast.

J: "I love you, Margaret."

M: (pause) "It's not enough, Jackson."

J: "Enough? For what? What do you mean?"

M: "I'm not sure. I can't see things clearly right now."

J: "So . . . you're saying you're in the dark . . . about *us*?"

M: "No. I think I'm saying that we're *all* in the dark about a lot of things."

J: "Speak for yourself, Margaret."

M: "OK. Then *I'm* in the dark."

J: "How dark is it?"

M: "Dark."

J: "Tell me *how* dark, Margaret."

M: "Pretty *fucking* dark, Jackson."

I don't know which is more selfish—wanting to be with Jackson or not wanting to be with him.

August 8
I'm a failure at love. That's what I told Tommy. And then he said he was happy for me. I said, "That's perverse. Why would you say that?" And he said, "Because you know that you *can* fall in love."

August 9
I think Jesus is too big for my small heart.

August 10
Is it pride that makes me not want to lose myself in another person?

August 11
Note: The word *pride* is located in the dictionary after *prick* and before *priest*.

PRIDE: 1. Too high of an opinion of oneself; conceit: *Pride goes before a fall.* 2. The best part; prime. 3. *Archaic.* High spirit; mettle. 4. *Obsolete.* Sexual desire in a female animal; heat. 5. A group (of lions).

Related observation: My mother, Stella, and I are all Leos.

August 12
I am eighteen years old today, so I feel pretty *good.* But Tommy has decided to tell Jackson that he's homosexual, so I feel pretty *bad.* Feeling bad makes me realize that I'm right not to be with Jackson, so that's good, *I guess,* depending on how you twist your mind around it.

August 13

Tommy & I went to a bar called Private Eyes—a sleazy place full of people who think they look great—and we walked in and Tommy went to find a table. I went straight to the bar and ordered a Jack Daniel's on the rocks. It was the first time I've ever legally ordered a drink and the bartender didn't even card me, so I was feeling very adult and in control. Then he handed me the drink & asked for $3.00 (which seemed steep) and gave me this round token after I paid. "What's this?" I asked. "You can get a free drink with that," he said, and I went to find Tommy. Thirty minutes later, the waitress comes to our table for another order, and I ask for another Jack Daniel's and I hand her my token.

"You can't use that," she said.

"Why?"

"Because only men can use tokens."

"But they gave me this at the bar and I paid $3.00 for my drink."

"Oh, you should've only paid $1.00. They must have thought you were buying a drink for a man."

We argued for a few useless minutes. I said, "Well, that stinks," and gave the token to Tommy, who ordered my drink for me.—The whole thing felt like a weird foreshadowing of my future life.

August 14

Around 6 o'clock, I walked into Tommy's kitchen after a jog and there were Jackson and Yvonne with Tommy. I said "Hello, everybody," and immediately went upstairs to Tommy's bathroom, where I confirmed that I looked like a red beet and smelled like a dead dog. I drank some water out of a glass on the counter. I gagged. There were *toenails* in the glass! I ran down the stairs yelling, "Tommy! I drank your toenails! I'm going to die of toenail poisoning!" Everyone looked up. Then we all laughed so hard we were crying.

August 15
Betsy has been writing from LSU but all she asks about is Tommy. Mitch called to complain that the most beautiful girls on campus won't look at him so he's miserable. At least I'm not the only one losing touch with reality.

August 16
Tommy left. It unnerved me. He said he wrote Jackson a letter a couple of days ago, because he couldn't continue to be friends with Jackson unless Jackson knew. I said, "Knew what?" He said, "That I'm a *fuckin' faggot, Maggie*!" Tommy's scared to death and so am I.

August 17
Elvis Presley died yesterday. I miss Angela terribly. No word from Jackson.

August 18
I went for a walk after dinner tonight, and Daddy asked to come along, which was different, but seemed nice. Then on the walk, he told me he has angina and that his arteries are clogged and it's possible he could have a heart attack one day. He made a point of being calm. He said he was telling me this because he was thinking of Mama and Sara and what would happen to them if anything happened to him. That was when I stopped breathing. Daddy looked me in the eye and told me I was not to worry, that he was fine, that he just wanted me to know in *case*. So I asked him what

he was going to do and he said, "I'm going to live my life, Margaret, and so are you."

August 19
A story in the Talmud: A son left his father. He was asked to return, but said "I can not return." Then the father sent a message to the son, "Return as far as you can, and I shall come the rest of the way."

August 20
Jackson came over to say good-bye. It was not a good conversation.

M: "Have you written Tommy?"
J: "I'm not sure *what* I'm going to do, Margaret. Let's not talk about it."
M: "But you're going to write to him?"
J: "*Don't* do this."
M: "Don't do *what?*"
J: "Argue. I know you and Tommy think this means I don't love him, but I do."
M: "I know you love Tommy. But if you think Tommy doesn't know that, then I suggest you *tell* him."
J: "Margaret! Listen. You know . . . I don't believe we can question the Bible just because what it says doesn't suit us."
M: "Are we talking about the Bible?"
J: "I am. And if you aren't, then this conversation isn't going to work."
M: "But why not?"
J: "God isn't the enemy here, Margaret."

M: "I don't think God is the enemy. I just want to talk about
   Tommy."

J: "You don't make anything easy."

M: "What do you mean?"

J: "I mean I don't think I can talk to you about *this.*"

Hmmmm. Right now, I'm thinking of that part in *Invasion of the
Body Snatchers* where the main character figures out that the people who *look* like his friends, really aren't, they're *aliens.* Now I
know how that feels.

August 21

My heart tells me not to be angry. My heart tells me that Jackson
has lost more than I have.

August 22

"Everything comes and goes, just like lovers & styles of clothes.
Things you held high and told yourself were true, start changing
when it all comes down to you." (Joni Mitchell)

August 23

Jesus wept—because Jesus knew.

August 24

I've failed, but there's a sense of freedom, too. The two emotions
overlap.

August 25

When I'm ready, I will to go to church, but only when the church is
empty. I'll read the Bible, but only the *red letters.* And I will pray,
but not with words.

August 26
Letter from Tommy. He says not to be upset for his sake. He says
an affair with a cowboy is a good idea and he wishes he'd thought
of it first.

August 27
In my dream, I run into Jackson and Yvonne in the Townsends'
driveway. It's awkward at first, but then we all begin talking and
it's OK. We're all feeling fine and there is a miraculous *niceness*.
Then Jackson says something about Tommy in passing, without
realizing that it offends me, and I don't know what to do. My eyes
meet Yvonne's eyes. That's when I know that *she* understands
that all the good feelings are on the verge of blowing apart.
And in that moment, I choose to *ignore* his remark because I suddenly grasp that my getting angry won't change anything and
would only create bitterness where I want there to finally be
peace. So I say good-bye, genuinely and kindly. And they say
good-bye, also with genuine kindness. And that was the end of
the dream.

The part of the dream that stays with me is the moment
in the driveway when Yvonne seemed deeper to me than Jackson,
when she and I shared an understanding that he didn't get.

August 29
(6:15 a.m.) Daddy is loading the car. Mama left me a note that
says, "Your absence will certainly leave this house a lot duller and
your parents and brother and sister, a little sad."—So, I just want to
put down here, in *this* diary, that I'm going to miss my family but
not much else—except maybe the levee and the river. But the river
will always be here, in this place, in the holy land of life so far. I'm

going to leave this diary *behind* so I can start a *new* one, when I get where I'm going.

"Bye Bye Miss American Pie . . . drove my Chevy to the levee but the levee was dry . . . and good old boys were drinking whiskey and rye, and singing this'll be the day that I die . . ."

What
Happened
Next

*A*FTER GRADUATING HIGH SCHOOL, I moved around a lot. I attended three universities, lived for a time in Paris, and graduated in 1981 from the University of North Carolina at Chapel Hill with a degree in English literature. Just over a year later, I married photographer and writer Alex Harris in a small, private ceremony surrounded by immediate family and close friends, including my parents, Momma Doll, Tommy, Jackson, and Yvonne. Aunt Lou was too ill to attend. Mitch, who during college became my good and dependable friend, lent me and my new husband the use of his apartment in New Orleans for our honeymoon. Only recently did I learn that Angela's absence from my wedding was due, at least in part, to the fact that my husband is Jewish.

Tommy Townsend received a master's degree in architecture from Princeton in 1984. After years of living and working in New

York City, Tommy moved back to the South in 1993 to open his own office of architecture and interior design in New Orleans. He lives there with his long-time partner Jeff, an environmental engineer, and their two cats. Tommy and I communicate on a weekly, if not daily, basis, as we have for decades, and his dinner parties are fabulous.

Jackson Bishop is an ordained pastor in the Presbyterian church. He and Yvonne are married and have three children. In 2003, Jackson led his 900-member congregation to break away from the mainstream church to join an evangelical family of churches. In an official newsletter, the departure was attributed to "a restlessness with regard to issues at the national level, such as the continuing debate over whether [the church] should ordain sexually active gays and lesbians."

Mitch Hardy became a medical doctor specializing in sports and emergency room medicine. Soon after finishing medical school, he helped found a successful professional corporation of physicians, and eventually that corporation was sold to a limited-liability HMO. Soon after, Mitch retired from full-time medicine. He, his wife, and their three children live in a community that allows for a quiet life and the pursuit of a variety of sports.

My cousin **Angela** met a young minister when she was nineteen. They married and have three children. Angela graduated from college with honors and a degree in Home Economics. She works as a substitute teacher and homemaker. Her husband, though originally called to a ministry in the Southern Baptist church, has for many years worked with independent nondenominational congregations. He is currently a church "planter" for a worldwide evangelical organization. Angela and I have seen one another only rarely since she married.

Betsy is a registered nurse, married, the mother of four sons, and is devoted to both family and church. **Wanda** lives with her husband and daughters, placing a high value on privacy and friends. **Pam** is divorced with three children. She is a successful painter who travels often and lives large.

Aunt Lou endured periods of severe depression for most of her adult life. She died in 1986 of an embolism that reached her brain.

My grandmother **Momma Doll** died of pneumonia in 1989. She suffered the slow ravages of Alzheimer's disease for more than a decade.

Mary and **Riley** live in Texas, where Mary manages the office of an orthodontist and Riley is an independent businessman. They have two daughters.

Stella and **Jim** married in 1979 and have two children. They divorced in 2002. Stella currently teaches art in the public schools.

Bill is an attorney at law with a practice based in Monroe. His wife, Mindy, also from Monroe, is an interior designer. They and their three children live within walking distance of the house where Bill and I grew up.

Sara currently lives, works, and paints in New York City. She had her first solo gallery show of paintings in New York in 2005.

**Daddy holding me on the day of my christening,
Easter Sunday 1960**

Tom Sartor died at home of a massive heart attack on March 11, 1984.

My mother, **Bobbie Sue**, remarried in 1998. She lives with her husband, Eugene, a retired businessman, in the house on the levee where I was raised. **Ellen Townsend** still lives next door.

Epilogue

*I*N MY MOST ENDURING MEMORIES OF GROWING UP, I am alone, or if not alone, then the images have a quality of solitary observation: the texture of my mother's hair, the sharp angles of Angela's body, the echo of my father's footsteps in the hospital corridor. It's easy for me to recall the dark protection of the carport during a summer downpour or to conjure the sweet stink of the river and the way the turtles popped up their heads through the murky water to watch me watch them.

We do not know ourselves. This is what I have learned. Having read through my diaries, my private past has taken on qualities it did not have before. For one thing, it's no longer private. Autobiography is necessarily limited by the mind's locked drawers and the author's skewed perspective, but putting it plainly, the girl in *my* story would have been nicer and wiser were it not for the misfortune of written evidence. The lives described in my diaries, including my own, are depicted only in part, imperfectly, and seen only through my adolescent eyes. What I chose to record begs the question, to me as much as anyone, of what I left out, and why. A question I can't fully answer. But to paraphrase the Apostle Paul: until the perfect comes, the parts will have to do.

Some of what is not recorded is amusing. I recall the ongoing struggle with my hair as a far more constant and ugly battle than it appears to be in the diary. When I hit puberty, my hair became a thick, tangled, unruly rope of braid that could not be undone in public without risking humiliation. I performed rituals involving hot irons and orange juice cans-cum-curlers in hopes of taming the beast, but there was no remedy that could not be undone by a hard rain. For years, I felt certain that if only I had silky Peggy Lipton hair, my whole life would go more smoothly. At fourteen, I carried a Breck shampoo ad to my first beauty parlor haircut, imagining myself as a girl with soft bangs that swept down over her forehead with a subtle flip. That day it was drizzling, and by the time I reached home, my new bangs were alive, springing off my forehead. For the next six months, they flew, whipped, and fuzzed, but they never ever flipped. I didn't cut my hair again until I was over thirty.

Some of the revelations were entirely unexpected. The icy psychiatrist, for instance, who, as it turns out, had me nailed. But astute psychological analysis and emotional healing do not always go hand in hand, and reading the shrink–patient dialogue (which I have no memory of recording) did nothing to alter my long-held impression that those sessions were no ointment to my angst.

Anxiety in an adolescent girl is a tricky business. At the outset of the diary, I was a garden-variety coward, confounded by my own misery, frightened of boys, and terrified of physical embarrassment. During high school, I weighed myself regularly, exercised constantly, and often connected the image in the glass with my fluctuating sense of self-worth. In other words, I was like every other teenage girl I knew. When I found religion, I discovered fasting as a means to spiritual clarity and since it was clarity I was seeking, this was a path I welcomed. Looking back at those years, I have some shame about the harsh demands I made on my growing body, but I feel genuine *anguish* over the pain suffered by friends right in front of my eyes, pain that I didn't even recognize, let alone try to alleviate. Despite that and other failures, I made a kind of progress. In my late teens, I was guarded and intense, but I was not a coward. With conscious effort, I moved towards a more constructive form of self-scrutiny and gradually developed elaborate strategies for managing my darker moods and doubts. By the time I left home, I was beginning to understand that the sense of clarity I sought in my life was not at all synonymous with simplicity, and that it never would be.

The diaries stirred me up. At the end of a day of reviewing and editing the material, immersed in a life that had been mine—but that felt both unfamiliar and weirdly accurate—I would sit at the kitchen table in my old farmhouse, with fresh flowers and mismatched silverware, and have dinner with my husband and two children. Sometimes I told them stories, but more often I tried to put my past aside and be an attentive spouse and parent, all the while with my heart racing and my fifteen-year-old self secretly inhabiting and twisting my thoughts.

My nights became restless. I would lie awake, composing letters of apology in my head for things I said, did, or wrote so many years ago that I could not actually summon, let alone explain, the reasons I had said, done, or written them. During one of those late-night guilt trips, I gained new perspective on an odd event that had happened in the mid-1980s: a phone call from Jackson. I was at home in North Carolina and Jackson was somewhere in Alabama. There was no animosity between us, but we were both married and had not been in touch for a long time. That morning, he tracked me down because he was convinced that an unsigned poem he'd found on his car in his church's parking lot had been left by me. It took a while to convince him otherwise, and when I did, I think we were both embarrassed and confused. I thought the whole thing a little nutty and inappropriate, but I was not offended. What I couldn't understand was the departure from logic that his assumption had required. I didn't understand it then, but I do now. Sometimes the past isn't past.

My own confusion between past and present, feelings and events, became apparent when, while reading the diaries, I decided to contact Jackson. My short e-mail was carefully crafted and matter-of-fact. Jackson's response, by contrast, was spontaneous and poignant. He looked back on our shared youth with tenderness, even awe. He referred to Tommy with affection and regret. My hasty reply was blunt. I was riled by Jackson's self-assurance *and* his sentimentality. For years, Jackson had taken a very public stance within his church against the ordination of homosexuals, and for me that translated into his saying that Tommy's life was an abomination. None of it added up, and for me, it doesn't still, but then who am I to cast stones? My ill-considered response was honest, but to Jackson, it must have seemed inappropriate. A boiling over of emotion can happen to any of us, and may be brought on by many things: a diary, a poem, a message, breakfast. Stir up the past and stuff spills out.

On the surface at least, in my note to Jackson I was defending Tommy, but there was more to it. Like a fast-acting form of psychoanalysis, the diaries had made me aware of many previously hidden well-springs of my adult personality. They had uncovered old wounds, losses that had formed me. "I am in hell but I am not dead," I wrote at the age of fifteen on the night of my first break-up with Jackson, and that is exactly how I remember it felt. Don't misunderstand. I know this was a minor event for the rest of the human race, including Jackson. There had been a drawn-out vagueness to our deepening intimacy. We weren't officially a couple and Jackson sent me his message that night through Tommy. Logically, in the face of the confusion I later caused in his life and in the lives of Mitch and Yvonne, the event should be deemed trivial. It was my private heartbreak. However, due to my complete inexperience in love, it was also the only one in my life for which I was *totally* unprepared. There are certain wounds that you don't get past, and instead, they define you. First heartbreak can be that kind of injury.

Through sheer force of will, I kept most of my late-night remorse and ranting within the confines of my own home and head. I rarely discussed the diary with anyone, except of course Tommy, with whom I discussed it constantly. My husband, Alex, did get an earful on a regular basis, but only Tommy was aware of everything, every upheaval in detail. Through e-mail and phone calls, he kept track of my movement. He listened and answered, confirmed and contradicted. He deciphered the clues right along with me. Only Tommy could give me license to keep at it, to continue my disruptive journey into the past, because we both knew that it was his story I was telling as well.

It was fair of me to assume that my long friendship with Tommy was also an alliance that put us on one side and Jackson firmly on the other. But when I traveled to New Orleans to retrieve the notes and letters I had written to Tommy during high school, I discovered more than I had planned. Staying with Tommy and his partner, Jeff, in their home in the French Quarter, I spent two full days taking notes on my laptop and digging through three paper grocery sacks full of letters that Tommy had recently retrieved from his childhood bedroom closet. As I went through the bags, I made three piles: letters from me, letters from Jackson, and letters from everyone else. All this I did in the privacy of an attic guest room while Tommy and Jeff were at work. At the end of the second day, I met Tommy at his office, and on the way home started talking about what I was doing.

Tommy parked his silver station wagon and we walked the short block to the ancient shotgun house. I was trotting to keep up with his long strides and speaking very quickly, excited about what I'd found. Tommy had saved not only my posted letters, but notes I'd left on his car and stuck through the vents in his school locker. He'd kept the silly poems I'd written for his birthdays. I was also very curious about the letters from Jackson, eager to see, in his own words, what Jackson would surely have confided in Tommy about our achingly drawn-out affair. I waited on the sidewalk as Tommy put his key in the heavy wooden door, and there was a noticeable pause before he turned it in the lock.

"You can't read Jackson's letters," he said.

We pushed through the doorway and into the narrow hall. Jeff wasn't home yet, and I heard the two cats padding rapidly down the steep staircase to beg for their dinner.

"Why on earth not?" I asked.

"Because I'd have to ask Jackson's permission to let you read them."

"His permission? You're kidding."

"No. I'm not."

There was resolve in Tommy's voice, and something else, too. He was protecting Jackson. I was incredulous.

"For goodness' sake, look what Jackson stands for and writes and preaches . . . his assurances that homosexuals will never be ordained? What about the Web site of that evangelical group his church joined . . . and what they say about the innocent victims of AIDS, versus the gay, *guilty* ones? Why would you protect him?"

"It just wouldn't be right."

That night after Jeff went to bed, Tommy and I talked until after three a.m. What amazed me as much as Tommy's unexpected loyalty to Jackson, was his lack of anger. He had not always been that way. After coming out, Tommy had felt ashamed, not for being gay, but for being so naive as to be duped into thinking that there was something wrong with being gay. So gradually that night, it was my own moral failure in an unfair world that became painfully obvious. While Jackson and I had both been freely handed the right to live our lives in full view of the world and the communities in which we lived, without inviting judgment, Tommy had no such right. He had been denied. Yet it was Tommy who was the first to turn the other cheek.

Friendships so deep as to seem miraculous are complicated. I can describe the twists and turns of this triangular love affair of my youth, but I can't say what they mean. The latest twist appears to be a turn towards reconciliation. The last time I visited Monroe, Tommy and Jeff were visiting there as well, and so were Jackson and Yvonne. It was early January 2005 and Jackson phoned Tommy to say that he and his wife wanted to see him, and to meet Jeff. So while Alex and I were next door in my mother's kitchen, Tommy and Jeff and Jackson and Yvonne sat with Ellen in her living room. It was a new year.

THE SHIFT FROM AN ADOLESCENT PERSPECTIVE to an adult one can be an adjustment akin to moving from shade to sunlight, or an effort tantamount to showing the blind how to see. The same story can be a different story depending on the perspective you bring to it. Or another way of thinking about this is: if I have a fight with my teenage son, it is always my fault, even when it is his fault. William will argue with me as though his survival depends on it, because maybe it does, because to him, it *feels* like it does. Point of view is a kind of truth. Growing up is a long process. The important thing to understand is that we are all just feeling our way.

It was my father's sudden heart attack that taught me that even our very deepest emotional connections are fragile, as are our very deepest emotions. My grief over his death released half a lifetime's worth of held-in tears. The only other means I have ever found to trigger emotions that out of reach—is stories.

When my daughter was in preschool, she would ask me over and over to read aloud from one particular book, the story of an old woman who sits on her porch and thinks about her childhood, her dead parents, and how she didn't know *then* that she should tell them things, things she is thinking now, now that she is an old woman sitting on her porch. Whenever I picked up this book, my nose began to sting, and by the second or third page, tears were rolling down my cheeks. I always choked out the final words with difficulty. It was exhausting, but Eliza was relentless. Even if I hid the book, which I did, she would rifle the bookcase to find it. So I read. I trembled and took deep breaths and my voice came out my nose. All of this fascinated my young daughter, but it was more than a little troubling to me. It is one thing to experience pain through one's own memories, for me to recall afternoons in Aunt Lou's kitchen or sewing with Momma Doll—to look at the photograph of my father holding me on the day of my christening, wearing his crisp bow tie and that subtle smile, my toddler fingertips reaching out to touch his broad open hand—but this was someone else's story. Or was it?

In the home that I occupy now, the stillness late at night is a small miracle. During the day, the energy that surrounds me is constant and explosive. When confronted by chaos, I still have a tendency to panic. Only now it's not God and school and boyfriends, but the overload of work, a house with children and various animals, the disturbing news on the radio, dirty dishes, and unanswered e-mail. The labyrinth of life will forever confuse me. But at two a.m., I can look into the bedrooms of my children and savor the awkward poses of their dreams, study their sighs and coughs. I can straighten the sheet gone askew and lift the quilt kicked to the floor. I can make things better. It's an old story, the oldest, but there *is* comfort in love. I am still an escapist at heart.

THERE ARE TIMES IN LIFE, and adolescence is surely one of them, when you have to take yourself more seriously, when the choices are more crucial and defining. In my youth, in so many ways, I failed, and the world failed me. But I also loved mightily, and was so loved in return. For me, the hard truth about growing up is that I lost something. By that, I don't mean a home or a person. What I'm trying to say is this: I lost the answers. And that may be what telling this story is all about.

I still pray, only now I mostly listen. And though some of what I hear is sad, some of it is lovely. Some of it became this book.

March 20, 2005
Alex and I went out for Chinese food tonight. After dinner, we broke open our cookies and his fortune was, "You will have good luck in your personal affairs." Mine read, "You think that is a secret, but it never has been one."

Sartor farm, Alto, Louisiana 2005

Acknowledgments

When I began reading my childhood diaries, I didn't intend to write a book, but as the idea of shaping the record of my adolescent experiences into a memoir began to emerge, certain colleagues, friends, and family members generously provided the support necessary for me to see this project through to completion.

Initially, Catalina Arocena, Geoff Dyer, and Rob Sikorski read abbreviated transcriptions of the diaries and their positive responses gave me the confidence to continue. My early attempts at a coherent manuscript were read by Laurie Cochenour, Ann Stewart, and Donna Zapf, and their feedback helped me to uncover the essential story I wanted to tell. Virginia Holman, Allan Gurganus, and Andrea Quarracino read later drafts at different stages and I benefited enormously from their insight and guidance on how to shape the book. Lee Smith's critical reading of the manuscript and her unflinching faith in the project were crucial. The day

Reynolds Price enthusiastically endorsed this book was the day I allowed myself to believe that I was on to something.

The staff at the Rare Book, Manuscript, and Special Collections Library at Duke University provided practical assistance, especially Robert Byrd and Linda McCurdy. The Duke University Institute of the Arts awarded me a professional development grant, making it possible for me to travel to New Orleans to retrieve old letters.

The photographs and journals of William Gedney were an inspiration to this project.

For their help, encouragement, and advice, I am indebted to Susan Graham, Gill Holland, Harry Hubenthal, T.S. Hubenthal, Tim Kirkman, Helen Ledbetter, Doug Meffert, William Noland, Kathy Pories, Shannon Ravenel, Polly Shteamer, Emily Sartor, F. W. Sartor, Nora Fredrick Sartor, Sandy Sartor, Anna Schriefer, and Daniel Wallace. And of course to the staff at Bloomsbury, including Benjamin Adams, Maya Baran, Nicola Ferguson, Amy King, and Greg Villepique.

Special thanks goes to my children, Eliza and William Harris, for their patience and genuine interest, and to my mother, who was enormously helpful and engaged in every way.

I wish that my father were alive to see this story published.

I am grateful to my talented agent, Emily Forland, whose suggestions were invaluable; to my editor, Colin Dickerman, who gently but masterfully guided this book to its final form; and to Lee Ledbetter, friend extraordinaire.

This book is dedicated, with love, to my husband, Alex Harris.

A Note on the Author

Margaret Sartor was born and raised in Louisiana. She currently lives with her husband, Alex Harris, and two children in Durham, North Carolina, where she teaches at the Center for Documentary Studies at Duke University. She is a photographer and the editor of three books, most recently (with Geoff Dyer) *What Was True: The Photographs and Notebooks of William Gedney*.

Reading Group Guide

Questions for Discussion:

1) What are the key personal and social issues raised by the story Margaret Sartor tells in her book? Though these events occurred decades ago, do any of these issues resonate now?

2) Margaret Sartor begins her book in January 1972, when she is "in the seventh grade at Robert E. Lee Junior High in Monroe, Louisiana, the United States of America, the Earth, the Universe," and immediately states she is bored out of her mind. Is Margaret's assessment of her life more indicative of her age or where she resides?

3) Margaret is best friends with her next-door neighbor, Tommy Townsend, who remains a close friend through her adulthood. How would this relationship be described?

4) What role does Momma Doll, Margaret's maternal grandmother, play in her life? What does she offer that Margaret's parents do not?

5) Margaret mentions that her sisters Mary and Stella "have baby books with lots of pictures and writing," that her baby book "has only three pictures," and that her brother, Bill, "doesn't even have a baby book." Does birth order have an impact on Margaret's self-esteem?

6) Horseback riding is a frequent activity for Margaret and she is very sensitive to the animals and pets that come and go in her life. Do animals fill any voids for her?

7) Do Margaret's keen observations about her family and friends have an impact on the level of anxiety she feels?

8) The school board in Margaret's town decides to integrate the two formerly segregated public high schools by requiring all ninth graders to attend the former predominantly white high school and all tenth graders to attend the previously all-black high school. Margaret's father assures her that people will get used to it. Margaret's mother appears to be more worried about sex and violence in movies than she is about desegregation of the schools. Are Margaret's parents more progressive than other residents of their town?

9) Margaret's Aunt Lou suffers from depression. How does this affect Margaret's family? Does Aunt Lou's illness influence the way Margaret views her own mental health?

10) In high school, Margaret meets Jackson Bishop, a handsome athlete whom she dates off and on for years. What bonds Margaret and Jackson? How is Margaret's relationship with Jackson different from her relationship with her other longtime beau, Mitch Hardy?

11) Margaret idolizes her cousin Angela and notes "It's scary how much I love her." Yet Margaret and Angela become distant as adults. What causes the split?

12) Margaret's parents have another baby, Sara, when her mother is forty-five years old and her father is fifty five. What impact does the newest member of the Sartor family have on Margaret?

13) Tommy Townsend, Margaret's best friend, reveals he is gay. Is their relationship changed by this disclosure?

14) Margaret is accepted at Trinity University in San Antonio, Texas as a President's Scholar. Why does she want to attend college far away from home?

15) Christianity plays an important role throughout Margaret's life, although her parents are not devoutly religious people. Why are questions of religious and moral responsibility so important to Margaret? Does her faith influence the decisions she makes?